T0016382

# THE **MINI** ROUGH GUIDE TO
# PORTO

**ROUGH GUIDES**

# YOUR TAILOR-MADE TRIP
## STARTS HERE

**Tailor-made trips and unique adventures crafted by local experts**

Rough Guides has been inspiring travellers for more than 35 years. Leave it to our local experts to create your perfect itinerary and book it at local rates.

Don't follow the crowd – find your own path.

## HOW ROUGHGUIDES.COM/TRIPS WORKS

**STEP 1** Pick your dream destination, tell us what you want and submit an enquiry.

**STEP 2** Fill in a short form to tell your local expert about your dream trip and preferences.

**STEP 3** Our local expert will craft your tailor-made itinerary. You'll be able to tweak and refine it until you're completely satisfied.

**STEP 4** Book online with ease, pack your bags and enjoy the trip! Our local expert will be on hand 24/7 while you're on the road.

## PLAN AND BOOK YOUR TRIP AT
## ROUGHGUIDES.COM/TRIPS

# HOW TO DOWNLOAD YOUR FREE EBOOK

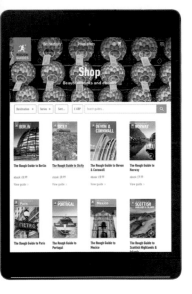

1. Visit **www.roughguides.com/free-ebook** or scan the **QR code** below

2. Enter the code **porto362**

3. Follow the simple step-by-step instructions

For troubleshooting contact: mail@roughguides.com

# **10** THINGS NOT TO MISS

**1**

**2**

**3**

**4**

**5**

**6**

**7**

1 **TORRE DOS CLÉRIGOS**
Porto's lofty landmark, with a 225-step climb up the Baroque tower for unrivalled views of the city. See page 44.

2 **PORT WINE CELLARS**
Tour the port cellars in Vila Nova de Gaia and sample Porto's most famous tipple. See page 66.

3 **THE SÉ**
Porto's imposing hilltop cathedral offers panoramic city vistas. See page 34.

4 **IGREJA DE SÃO FRANCISCO**
The austere church facade belies a breathtaking interior adorned with Baroque gilded woodcarving. See page 33.

5 **PALÁCIO DA BOLSA**
Historic home of the stock exchange, with an opulent interior. See page 32.

6 **JARDIM DO PALÁCIO DE CRISTAL**
Romantic gardens, with sensational views of the Douro. Kids will love the strutting peacocks and look-out turret. See page 57.

7 **ESTAÇÃO DE SÃO BENTO**
The arrival hall of Porto's central station is plastered with around 20,000 blue-and-white *azulejos* (tiles) depicting scenes from the city's history. See page 41.

8 **LELLO**
One of the world's most beautiful bookshops, thought to be the inspiration for Hogwarts in the *Harry Potter* novels. See page 46.

9 **SERRALVES**
An excellent contemporary art museum and Art Deco mansion in serene park surrounds. See page 64.

10 **CITY OF BRIDGES**
Languid one-hour river cruises putter beneath the magnificent bridges that straddle the Douro. See page 73.

# A PERFECT DAY

### 9am

**Breakfast.** Kick off the day with coffee, eggs and croissants at *Mercador Café* in Rua das Flores, an appealing street lined with handsome mansions and enticing shops.

### 10am

**Top of the tower.** Visit the nearby Clérigos Church (see page 44). Take a peek inside the beautiful Baroque interiors, then climb the 225 steps up the tower for unparalleled views of the city.

### 11am

**A feast of azulejos.** Duck down Rua dos Clérigos for the Praça da Liberdade, the civic heart of the city. The broad Avenida dos Aliados stretches grandly up to the Town Hall. Beyond the Praça you'll discover the São Bento railway station, its entrance hall bedecked with 20,000 *azulejos* (tiles) illustrating scenes from Portuguese history.

### Noon

**Sé to Ribeira.** Walk down the main street for the Sé and take in the sweeping city views from the esplanade. Admire the cathedral and cloisters before heading down the steps to the right of the Episcopal Palace. A stairway leads all the way to the Ribeira waterfront but if you run out of steam, a free lift makes light work of the steepest section.

### 1pm

**Quayside cafés.** From the Ribeira cross the Dom Luís I bridge to Vila Nova de Gaia. Take your pick from the clutch of river-view cafés or grab a gourmet snack to go from the Mercado Beira Rio just back from the waterfront.

# IN PORTO

### 2pm

**Port galore.** After lunch, sign up for a tour and tasting in one of the city's iconic port wine cellars (see page 67).

### 3.30pm

**Hilltop gardens.** Take the cable car up to the Jardim do Morro for spectacular views of the Douro, Ponte de Dom Luís I and pastel-hued Ribeira – and even more spectacular ones if you continue to the Serra do Pilar Monastery.

### 4.30pm

**Culture vulture.** Head to the museums of WOW Porto (see page 70), which span everything from Portuguese wine and history to cork, chocolate and fashion.

### 5.30pm

**Aperitivo time.** Hotfoot it back to Porto and stroll along the scenic Ribeira quayside. Pause for a *porto tónico* at one of the pavement cafés, gazing out over the port lodges clustered along the left bank.

### 8pm

**Trusty tavern.** Feast on local specialities at *Adega de São Nicolau* (see page 108), a cosy cellar restaurant at the western end of Cais da Ribeira. Try the cod cakes followed by *tripas à moda do Porto* (Port-style tripe).

### 10pm

**Hit the galerias.** Mingle with the locals in the bar-packed streets fanning out from Rua da Galeria de Paris, then party into the early hours at LGBTQ favourite *Café au Lait* or city stalwart *Plano B*.

# CONTENTS

OVERVIEW                                                                    10

HISTORY AND CULTURE                                                         16

OUT AND ABOUT                                                               27

**Ribeira**                                                                27
Cais da Ribeira 28, Ponte Dom Luís I 29, Casa do Infante 30, Palácio da Bolsa 32, Igreja
de São Francisco 33

**The Sé and around**                                                      34
The Sé 34, Terreiro da Sé 36, Paço Episcopal 36, Casa-Museu Guerra Junqueiro 37, Igreja
de Santa Clara 38

**Baixa (Downtown)**                                                       39
Avenida dos Aliados 40, Estação de São Bento 41, Praça da Batalha 41, Rua de Santa
Catarina 42, Mercado do Bolhão 43, The Clérigos Complex 44, Livraria Lello 46, Centro
Português de Fotografia 48, Rua das Flores 50

**Miragaia and Massarelos**                                                52
Riverside Miragaia 52, Museu Nacional de Soares dos Reis  55, The Arts Block 56, Jardins
do Palácio de Cristal 57, Along the waterfront 59

**Boavista and Serralves**                                                 61
Casa da Música 61, Market, cemetery and synagogue 62, Fundação Serralves 64

**Vila Nova de Gaia**                                                      66
Port wine lodges 67, The riverfront 70, Mosteiro da Serra do Pilar 71

**Excursions**                                                            72
Cantinho das Aromáticas 73, Six Bridges cruise 73, Foz do Douro and Matosinhos 75,
Afurada 80, Douro Valley 82

THINGS TO DO                                                               85
**Entertainment**                                                          85
**Shopping**                                                               88

**Children's Porto**     **93**
**Outdoor pursuits**     **94**

## FOOD AND DRINK     `98`

## TRAVEL ESSENTIALS     `115`

## WHERE TO STAY     `135`

## INDEX     `142`

## HIGHLIGHTS

The River Douro     13
Port and the British factor     20
Important dates     25
The Feitoria Inglesa     31
A feast for the eyes     42
Nicolau Nasoni     47
A port entrepreneur     68
Bridge climbing     75
Leça da Palmeira     80
The longest night of the year     96
What's on     97
Porto's sandwich special     105

## A NOTE TO READERS

At Rough Guides, we always strive to bring you the most up-to-date information. This book was produced during a period of continuing uncertainty caused by the Covid-19 pandemic, so please note that content is more subject to change than usual. We recommend checking the latest restrictions and official guidance.

# OVERVIEW

Portugal's second city has long been synonymous with port. Centuries ago, British merchant ships would cluster in Porto's medieval harbour to cart the region's eponymous wines back home. Today, you're more likely to see river-cruise boats tracing the contours of the Douro, puttering past the string of old port lodges that offer tours and tastings. But there's so much more to Porto than its famous ruby-red tipple. The former industrial hub is undergoing a cultural renaissance, as a wave of inventive chefs, artists and designers breathe new life into the city's old-world appeal. High-profile concerts pack out the Casa da Música, exciting art galleries flank Rua de Miguel Bombarda, and hip bars and pavement restaurants crowd the Ribeira waterfront.

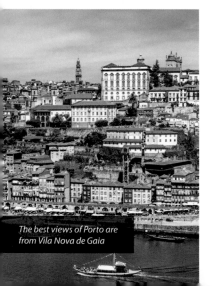

The best views of Porto are from Vila Nova de Gaia

## LOCATION, LOCATION

Much of the city's appeal lies in its location: a hillside sprawl tumbling down to the River Douro at the point where it pours into the Atlantic. Ever since the Romans established a trading route, Porto has prospered from commerce. It was here that Prince Henry the Navigator (1394–1460) learned his love of ships and initiated Portugal's role as one of the primary players in the Age of Discovery. Porto, where some of the caravels were built, thrived from the new sources of wealth. Later, the port wine trade with Britain was to compensate for the loss of the lucrative spice trade. Today the city is still the core of the port wine industry, and continued English involvement can be seen in the conspicuous names of the shippers and brands above the port wine lodges.

## HISTORIC PORTO

With its spectacular bridges, Baroque churches and eighteenth-century townhouses, Porto contains an enticing medley of architecture. Looming above the sea of red clay roofs, the Sé (Cathedral) and the 75m-high Torre de Clérigos pierce the skyline to dramatic effect. The city sweeps down vertiginous slopes to the banks of the Douro, with myriad *miradouros* framing superb views across the river to sister city Vila Nova de Gaia, where the old port wine cellars nurture the precious nectar.

Down on the waterfront is the Unesco-listed Ribeira quarter, where pastel-hued houses hook around the river, and pavement cafés spill out on to the cobblestones. Behind, a tangle of narrow alleys conceals hole-in-the-wall bars and tiny traditional restaurants. Renovation and gentrification may be underway, but this historic corner of the city still retains its authentic medieval character. Linking Ribeira with Vila Nova de Gaia is the great swoop of the Ponte Dom Luís I, the most central and iconic of the city's six bridges straddling the River Douro.

## PORTO VS LISBON

According to an old Portuguese saying *'Porto works while Lisbon plays, Coimbra studies and Braga prays'*. Porto is proud of its mercantile heritage and the fact that it gives its name not only to the famous fortified wine but also to the nation (it was called Portus Cale, the port of Cale, by the Romans – which gave rise to

*Unesco-protected Ribeira Square*

Portucale and hence Portugal). The city has always worked hard, and it is still a major commercial centre. The work ethic could have something to do with the climate. Porto lies in northwest Portugal, 314km north of Lisbon and only 3km from the Atlantic. While palm trees and bird-of-paradise flowers flourish on its hillsides, it has a cooler climate than Lisbon (heat waves are rare) and the rains are quite abundant (1,150mm per year), especially from November to March.

Like Lisbon, Porto is clustered on hills overlooking a river, but unlike the capital, with its pastel walls and Mediterranean light, Porto is in many ways a northern European city, with granite buildings (though softened by red-tile roofs) and hidden Baroque treasures. It is grittier and less polished than Lisbon, but is catching up with the capital fast, particularly when it comes to cuisine, hotels and shopping. Long regarded as Lisbon's quieter sibling, the city is known as 'the capital of the north', and with a population of just under 238,000 (or 2.4 million including the metropolitan area) it is the second-largest city in Portugal.

## PORTO'S RENAISSANCE

Just twenty years ago, Porto had a reputation for being closed and mysterious; its deserted centre a barren cultural landscape. In recent years, however, the city has seen a dramatic transformation, with spruced-up streets and a new sense of vitality. This increasingly cosmopolitan city is now a centre of arts, fashion and nightlife, with an undeniably youthful vibe. New bars and restaurants seem to open daily, along with a growing crop of hostels, hotels and Airbnbs to cater for the ever-increasing number of visitors. Art is no longer restricted to the treasures in museums and

### THE RIVER DOURO

Wending all the way from northern Spain, the River Douro has long been the source of Porto's wealth. It is the third-longest river of the Iberian Peninsula, flowing 900km (559 miles) from its source, near Duruelo de la Sierra in Spain, to the Atlantic at Porto. Upstream from the city the river winds through the steep and scenic terraced vineyards of the Douro Valley, famous for the country's centuries-old port. Traditionally the wine was shipped in oak barrels on *barcos rabelos* (flat-bottomed, square-sailed boats) to be stored in the cool port-wine lodges of Vila Nova de Gaia, across the river from Porto. This was a hazardous journey, with *rabelos* having to navigate the often shallow, fast-flowing waterways of the Upper Douro. These colourful craft are no longer used commercially (the wine is now transported, less romantically, by truck) but you can often see replica *rabelo* boats on the quayside in Porto, with wine barrels on board.

churches: dozens of cutting-edge galleries pepper the city's hip art neighbourhood, while eye-catching murals are splashed across the streets of previously abandoned quarters. There is a great music scene, a burgeoning festival programme and modern architecture galore. The culinary landscape is flourishing too, with Michelin-starred restaurants and trendy tapas bars wedged between traditional tavernas.

It's hardly surprising that Porto is a city-break favourite, frequently scooping the accolade of European Best Destination in trade magazines. The airport has been expanded to cater for direct flights from North America and Canada, and there are dozens of flights with low-cost carriers from other European cities. The award-winning cruise terminal at the port of Leixöes is also churning out ever greater numbers of visitors.

*Matosinhos beach*

But at the same time Porto still has the feel of a provincial city, known above all for its labyrinthine streets, hand-painted *azulejos* (tiles) and the occasional ornate architectural flourish. Vintage trams still rattle along its steep lanes, laundry flutters above crumbling facades, and old-timers still wash down huge plates of beans and tripe with port wine in the older cafés. Porto may have changed with the times,

> ### 'Porto' or 'Oporto'?
>
> If you want to sound like a local call the city 'Porto'. This has always been the local name but during the heady days of the port wine trade the British called it Oporto. The added 'O' is just the article which is placed before the name Porto, but the British thought it was part of the name and called it Oporto.

but the city hasn't lost its old-world charm along the way.

## BEYOND THE CITY

Monuments to former splendours, a beautiful cityscape and a signature tipple are not the end of the city's charms. From Porto you can visit the upper reaches of the Douro Valley, following the river on the trail of the chugging wine boats or taking the scenic rail route. You might like to hire a car and stay a night or two at one of the *quintas* (wine estates) to tour the vineyards and wineries.

Also within easy reach by rail or car are the historic cities of Braga and Guimarães in northern Portugal and, to the south, the university city of Coimbra. Then there's the seaside, just down the road, with sweeping views of the ocean and surfers.

A vintage tram trundles alongside the river to Foz do Douro where the river meets the ocean, or a bus or metro will whisk you to Matosinhos for gorgeous sunsets and the freshest of fish.

# HISTORY AND CULTURE

The Porto region has been inhabited for over three millennia, but it was the Romans who established the city of Portus on the right bank of the River Douro, and Cale facing it across the water. These twin cities gave rise to the dialect name 'Portucale', the origin of 'Portugal'; Porto is the city that gave its name to the nation as well as to the well-known fortified wine.

## EARLY SETTLERS

Since the days of the first settlers the fortunes of Porto have been linked with its location at the mouth of the River Douro where it empties into the Atlantic. The earliest recorded settlers were of

Azulejos depict Henrique conquering the Moors

Celtic origin and a few relics of their civilization have been discovered in the heart of Porto; otherwise, there are scant signs of early dwellers. Under Roman rule from the second century BC the city played an important role on the main trade route between Lisbon and Braga.

With the collapse of the Roman Empire, barbarian tribes invaded from northern Europe. In the fifth century the Germanic Suevi (Swabians) settled in Galicia, ruling from Braga and annexing much of the peninsula. Suevi rule was superseded by the Visigoths in 469, and control of the region changed once again in 711 when the Moorish invasion overwhelmed most of the Iberian peninsula. The Christian War of Reconquest of the peninsula (the Reconquista in Portuguese) began in 718 and took root in the north. By 868 Portucale was established as a frontier against Muslim rule by the Christian warlord, Count Vimara Peres, who held sway over the entire area between the Minho to the north and the River Douro.

## BIRTH OF A NATION

When Moorish power waned, 'Portucale' was just a small country of the Kingdom of León and Castile, centred on the Douro. It became independent after Afonso Henriques, the son of Henry of Burgundy, defeated the Moors at the Battle of Ourique in 1139 and named himself the first king of Portugal, Afonso I. By now he had captured Santarém and Lisbon, making his now royal realm the whole of present-day Portugal north of the River Tagus.

The legitimate male line of Henry of Burgundy finally ended in 1385 when João of Avis, known as João the Good, won a decisive victory against the Castilians at the famous Battle of Ajubarrota, assuring him as King of Portugal and a new ruling dynasty. King João's troops had been assisted by English archers and the victory prompted the Treaty of Windsor in 1386, the diplomatic Anglo-Portuguese alliance. This was well and truly sealed when the king married Philippa of Lancaster, daughter of John of Gaunt. The wedding took place with great pomp and ceremony in the cathedral of Porto and the alliance remains the oldest of its kind in the world.

## HENRY THE NAVIGATOR

King João and Philippa's fourth son, Henrique (1394–1460), was to change the map of the world. He is believed to have been born in Porto in the building now known as the Casa do Infante (House of the Prince, open to the public; see page 30). Known to the English as Henry the Navigator, he was famed as the founder and financier of Portugal's golden age of discovery. The launching point of his career was the daring capture of the Muslim North African city of Ceuta in 1415, with his father and brothers, putting an end to attacks by Barbary pirates on the Portuguese coast. For the venture against the Moors the people of Porto surrendered their finest cuts of meats to the navy and lived on tripe instead, thus earning them the nickname of *Tripeiros* or Tripe-eaters.

Henry was not, in fact, a navigator, but under his patronage Portuguese seamen founded the country's first colonies. In 1418 he moved south and established a school of navigation at Sagres, the desolate promontory in the southwest (the western tip of today's Algarve). Here he assembled a group of cartographers, astronomers, geographers and navigators to plot a sea route from Europe to India. Henry died in 1460 without finding the route to India, but Vasco da Gama's legendary sea voyage in 1497–99 paved the way for the Portuguese to establish their empire in Asia. The motivation for these voyages was partly religious, but largely commercial. By the time of his death in 1460 Henry had managed to establish a monopoly on all trade, including slavery, conducted along the African coast south of Cape Bojador.

In 1578 tragedy struck and altered the course of Portuguese history. The young King Sebastião was one of thousands killed at the

*Tripas à moda do Porto is still one of the city's iconic dishes*

Battle of Alcácer Quibir in a doomed attempt to invade Morocco. The death of the king led to the end of the Avis dynasty; Spain invaded in 1580, and it took 60 years for the Portuguese to organize a successful uprising against the occupation.

On 1 December 1640 – a date still celebrated as Portugal's Independence Day – Spanish rule was overthrown and the Duke of Bragança was crowned King João IV. His grandson, João V, enjoyed a long and glittering reign (1705–50), with wealth pouring in from gold discoveries in Brazil. It was during this time that many of Porto's church interiors were adorned with lavishly gilded woodwork.

## NAPOLEONIC INVASIONS

In Porto, as in the rest of Portugal, the Peninsular War and its aftermath halted progress for nearly half a century. During the three Napoleonic invasions, French troops took Porto twice, in 1808 and 1809; on the second occasion they were expelled by troops under the command of Arthur Wellesley, later the Duke of Wellington. On 29 March 1809 hundreds of fleeing residents drowned when the pontoon bridge across the Douro collapsed beneath their weight.

The Portuguese royal family had fled to Brazil in 1807, ahead of Napoleon's invading forces. At the end of the war King João VI declined to return to Portugal, triggering a complex series of political events and the 'War of the Two Brothers' in 1832–34, a fight for the Portuguese Crown between Miguel I for the Absolutists and Pedro IV (previously Emperor of Brazil) for the Liberals. Miguel

## PORT AND THE BRITISH FACTOR

Some say port was invented by British merchants looking to replace French claret, which was boycotted during wars with France in the seventeenth century. By adding a little brandy to the local red Douro, they found the wine sufficiently fortified to withstand temperature changes and long sea voyages. It also produced a fresh, sweet flavour that deepened with age. Whoever invented it, port was a big hit with the British and became 'as British as roast beef'. The Methuen Treaty of 1703 opened English markets to Portuguese wines, and the British shippers of Porto became increasingly rich and powerful. The next 30 years saw an unprecedented boom in trade in the Upper Douro and in 1727 a Shippers' Association was established to regulate the trade and control prices paid to the Portuguese producers. The explosion in trade gave rise to the famous port wine lodges spread over the hills of Vila Nova de Gaia. To combat the English stranglehold, the King of Portugal's Chief Minister, later the Marquês de Pombal, founded the Douro Wine Company in 1757 which restored a measure of Portuguese control. The Douro Valley became the world's first wine region with a legal demarcation, and Porto and its region a main engine room of Portuguese expansion and commerce.

and his troops besieged the Liberals in Porto for over a year. The war resulted in Miguel's exile and the restoration of liberalism, but further political strife followed. In September 1836 a democratic Chartists' group, which became known as the Septemberists, seized power but in turn split, with a royalist faction holding Lisbon and a republican junta holding Porto. A combined British and Spanish force, supporting the Quadruple Alliance of England, France, Spain and a royalist Portugal, received the surrender of the Porto junta in 1847.

*Port became 'as British as roast beef'*

## REGENERATION

In the second half of the nineteenth century, Porto crested a wave of economic revival, industrialization and urban expansion. The population soared as thousands of Portuguese from rural areas flocked to the city. The first Industrial Exhibition of the Iberian Peninsula was held in 1865 at Porto's original Palácio de Cristal, a building inspired by London's Crystal Palace. The creation of an ornate stock exchange, the Palacio da Bolsa, nods to the wealth of the city at the time. To keep up with growth, transport services were revitalized. In 1876 the French architect Gustav Eiffel designed the first railway bridge across the River Douro, the Ponte de Dona Maria Pia. Ten years later Eiffel's former partner, Théophile Seyrig, sketched the plans that were transformed into the iconic

Dom Luís I bridge. Towards the end of the century, electric trams were trundling through Porto.

## FROM REPUBLIC TO REVOLUTION

In 1908 the reigning Portuguese king, Carlos I, and his eldest son, Luís Filipe, were assassinated in Lisbon. Two years later, a republican revolution overthrew the monarchy. Portugal's last king, Manuel II, fled to England where he lived in exile, ending more than 750 years of monarchy. During the establishment of the Republic, Porto sustained its own democratic and republican leanings, and following the 1926 military coup, Porto was the centre of liberal opposition to Salazar's lengthy dictatorship, which lasted until 1968. The city declined in the 1960s; many citizens deserted Porto in favour of Foz do Douro or Matosinhos on the coast. Houses and buildings fell to disarray.

*The assassination of King Carlos I*

Porto metro travelling over the Dom Luís I bridge

The peaceful Carnation Revolution of 1974, led by army officers disaffected by the colonial wars in Africa, finally drew a line under the totalitarian regime. A period of great celebration ensued as Portugal emerged from decades of insularity. The years that followed were a mix of euphoria and political chaos.

## MODERN PORTO

Hot on the heels of joining the European Community in 1986, Portugal became one of the fastest growing countries in Europe. Ten years later, Porto received a boost with the designation of its historic centre as a Unesco World Heritage Site. The city was on a roll: it scooped the much-coveted title of European Capital of Culture in 2001, sparking a cultural resurgence, from the opening of the avant-garde Casa da Música to the regeneration of squares and streets. The good fortune wasn't to continue. Portugal's economy began to stagnate and the 2008 financial crisis left the country

## The Prime Minister's port

Port used to be given as a remedy for ailments. William Pitt the Younger (1759-1806), Britain's youngest Prime Minister, was a frail child and suffered gout from the age of 14. His doctor prescribed a bottle of port a day and Pitt continued to drink it throughout his life – which might explain why he died at the age of 47.

reeling, with a budget deficit fast spiralling out of control. In 2011 it became the third EU country after Greece and Ireland to ask for a financial bail-out from the EU. It wasn't until 2014, after a series of harsh austerity measures, that Portugal exited the bail-out programme. Slowly emerging from the shadow of recession, the national mood was buoyed further by the Portuguese football team winning the Euro 2016 in France. Tourism has given Portugal a big economic boost in recent years, and accounts for around 10 percent of GDP.

Porto sees fewer tourists than Lisbon or the Algarve, but in 2017 it was voted by travellers and tourism experts as Europe's Best Destination for the third time (also 2012 and 2014). As Porto has soared in popularity, concerns have flipped to overtourism. A city tax of €2 per person was added to overnight stays in accommodation in 2018, to alleviate any ill effects of excess tourism. No one, however, could have anticipated travel would nosedive so dramatically in 2020 when Covid-19 swept across the world. Travel restrictions to Portugal were eased in 2021 and visitor numbers recovered to 5.9 million, a year after plummeting to 3.9 million – the worst results since the mid-1980s. Though tourism rebounded quickly from the pandemic slump, an instant return to the record 16.4 million visitors of 2019 is unlikely, and it remains to be seen whether further restrictions will be put in place if coronavirus cases spike.

# IMPORTANT DATES

**140BC** Romans occupy the region and later found Portus Cale.

**5th century AD** Occupation by Visigoths.

**711** Moors conquer the peninsula.

**883** Northern Portugal (Portucale) regained by Christian forces.

**1143** Portucale becomes the new Kingdom of Portugal. Afonso Henriques is the first king of Portugal.

**1387** Dom João I and Philippa of Lancaster marry in the city's cathedral.

**1415** Conquest of Ceuta under Henry the Navigator. Explorers reach Madeira, starting the Age of Discoveries.

**1580** Portugal falls under Spanish rule for 60 years.

**1703** Methuen Treaty between Portugal and England, which becomes known as the 'Port Wine Treaty'.

**1808 / 1809** Napoleonic troops take Porto twice and are finally driven out in 1809 by Sir Arthur Wellesley (the future Wellington) in 1809.

**1832–33** Siege of Porto.

**1886** Opening of the Ponte Dom Luís I.

**1887** Opening of Gustave Eiffel's Ponte Maria Pia railway bridge.

**1891** Portugal's first republican revolution takes place in Porto.

**1910** Creation of the Portuguese Republic.

**1974** Carnation Revolution; end of Salazar's 48yr fascist dictatorship.

**1986** Portugal joins the European Community (now EU).

**1996** Ribeira granted Unesco World Heritage Site status.

**2001** Porto awarded title of European Capital of Culture.

**2004** Estádio do Dragão is built.

**2015** Award-winning cruise terminal opens at Leixões; Socialist leader António Costa becomes prime minister.

**2016** Social Democrat Marcelo Rebelo de Sousa becomes president. Portuguese football squad wins Euro 2016 tournament in France.

**2019** Portugal wins the UEFA Nations League at Estádio do Dragão, Porto.

**2020** Covid-19 halts tourism in Portugal and around the world.

**2021–22** Travel restrictions to Portugal ease, and tourism picks up again.

**2022** Costa's Socialist Party wins a rare majority government in elections.

Igreja de São Ildefonso

# OUT AND ABOUT

Lisbon's quieter sibling isn't about rushing around attempting to tick off honey-pot attractions from a must-see list. It's a city for meandering, a place for losing yourself in narrow alleyways not marked on maps and stumbling across an *azulejo*-splashed wall mural or a dinky traditional shop. The pace is unhurried: pause at a pavement café and linger over a *cimbalino* (espresso) and *pasteis de nata* – much-needed fuel for tackling the city's steep hills. Landmarks like the omnipresent River Douro and skyline-piercing Torre dos Clérigos will help you to reorientate yourself, or a friendly local will always point you in the right direction.

That's not to say Portugal's second city is short on culture: most of the galleries and museums are packed into the historic old town. For visits to the cellars of the old port wine lodges, you can simply cross the Dom Luís I bridge spanning the River Douro. Outlying attractions are easily reached by public transport; if the coastal lure of Foz do Douro beckons, for instance, you only have to hop on a bus or vintage tram.

The city is a perfect weekend getaway, but if you want to stroll through sleepy streets, savour seafood dinners and learn about ruby and tawny ports, give it another day or two and drink it all in slowly.

## RIBEIRA

Awarded Unesco World Heritage Site status in 1996, **Ribeira** (or Riverside) was one of the first areas of Porto to be inhabited. It was the city's original trade hub, with boats spitting out their merchandise on the quayside. Today it is Porto at its most picturesque: ancient arcades, candy-coloured houses and labyrinthine alleys. The river trade nowadays is purely for tourists, from one-hour cruises to see the 'city of bridges' to week-long trips up the Douro.

## CAIS DA RIBEIRA

Like many areas of Porto, the **Cais da Ribeira** – or River Quayside – was not so long ago a crumbling and rundown quarter. Now it's vibrant and colourful, with a string of river-view restaurants built into the arches of the old city walls. It's easy to while away the hours at café terraces, watching the world go by, or dining alfresco looking across to the twinkling lights of Vila Nova de Gaia. The hub of the waterfront is the Renaissance-era **Praça da Ribeira** ❶ (Ribeira Square), dominated by the *Pestana Vintage Porto* hotel and packed with riverside bars. Towards the back of the square is a 1970s fountain with a large bronze, corner-balanced cube, with sculpted pigeons on its sloping sides. Behind it is the eighteenth-century Fonte da Rua de São João (Fountain of St John) with a modern twist: the statue of São João – patron saint of the city – was later added in the niche. To the west of the square, Rua da Fonte Taurina, one of the oldest streets in the city, is lined by hole-in-the-wall tavernas.

At the eastern end of the Cais da Ribeira, just before the open archway, is a bronze relief commemorating the Ponte Das Barcas tragedy on 29 March 1809, when the pontoon bridge across the river collapsed beneath the weight of people fleeing from Napoleon's troops. Hundreds of citizens are thought to have drowned, and candles are still lit here in their memory. Through the arch (but not signed) is the **Ascensor da Ribeira** (Ribeira Lift, also known as the Elevador de Lada; daily 8am–8pm, shorter hours in winter; free), which whisks you up the hillside through the ramshackle **Barredo** quarter to Rua de Lada. Alternatively, you can climb the calf-shredding slopes through this characterful neighbourhood, and on to the Cathedral quarter.

# PONTE DOM LUÍS I

Built in 1880–86 to link Porto with sibling city Vila Nova de Gaia on the south bank of the river, the 172m-high **Ponte Dom Luís I ❷** (or Ponte Luís I) was the work of Portuguese engineer Teófilo Seyrig, the former business partner of Gustav Eiffel. The previous bridge was the Ponte Pênsil, and you can still see two granite piers which once supported it. Today's bridge, which forms the backdrop of many a postcard and photo, is a bold, two-tiered iron structure. Both levels are accessible on foot; the lower is also open to cars, the upper to the metro. It is well worth crossing Ponte Dom Luís I for the far-reaching views of Porto, Gaia and the **Dona Maria Pia Bridge** (1875–77) upstream, which was designed by Eiffel himself. If you're continuing to Gaia, take the upper tier for the Monastery, the lower one for the port wine lodges.

*The mighty Ponte Dom Luís I*

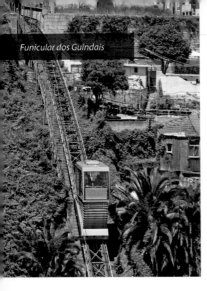
*Funicular dos Guindais*

Still on the Porto side of the river, just beyond the bridge, the **Funicular dos Guindais** (every 10min April–Oct Mon–Thurs & Sun 8am–10pm, Fri & Sat 8am–midnight; Nov–March Mon–Thurs & Sun 8am–8pm, Fri & Sat 8am–midnight) links the quayside with Batalha in the upper part of the city. A funicular has operated here on and off since 1891. The latest incarnation, dating back to 2004, is a swish and contemporary affair, which shuttles you up (or down) the hillside in a couple of minutes.

## CASA DO INFANTE

Ribeira's main monuments lie inland from the waterfront on the western side. Just north of the Largo do Terreiro is the **Casa do Infante** ❸ (House of the Prince; Tues–Sun 10.30am–1pm & 2.30–5.30pm; free at weekends), reputedly the birthplace in 1394 of the Infante Dom Henrique, better known as Henry the Navigator, who launched Portugal's age of discovery. The building is an old customs house, which was created in 1325 and functioned for over 500 years, with a mint also established on site. The tower was the main royal building in the city and it is believed that João I and his wife Philippa of Lancaster, who were married in Porto, lived here during their long stay in the city. Henry was their fourth and last surviving son. Today, an interpretive centre features an exhibition on Henry and the New World, with particular emphasis on the role of Porto. Little remains of the original building, but there are reconstructed sections of the original customs house and mint within the museum, as well as a piece of mosaic flooring from Roman times discovered in the foundations.

Henry the Navigator is omnipresent in this quarter. Cross the Rua Infante Dom Henrique for the eponymous *praça* (square), dominated by a statue of Henry, poised high on a pedestal pointing towards the sea. Looming above the northern side of the square is the conspicuous red iron **Mercado Ferreira Borges**, built to replace the old Ribeira market and now home to the **Hard Club** (www.hardclubporto.com), a huge cultural venue offering a dynamic programme of events at wallet-friendly prices. It

## THE FEITORIA INGLESA

Designed by the British Consul John Whitehead and built in 1785–90, the Feitoria Inglesa or English Factory House was created as an exclusive meeting place for British port merchants and financed entirely by their annual contributions. You can't miss the building – a huge neo-Palladian structure on what was previously called the Rua dos Ingleses (Street of the English), where it crosses Rua de São João. From 1811 it became the headquarters of the British Association, set up to promote port and keep traditions alive. Today it is still owned and run by the English port wine companies and hosts traditional social events accompanied, of course, by the fortified wine (needless to say, the collection of vintage bottles is priceless). A traditional Wednesday lunch still takes place when members and their guests have blind tastings of vintage port. Decorated with chandeliers, Chippendale furniture, porcelain and silverware, the rooms retain their grandeur. The Feitoria is closed to the public but if you happen to know a member it is well worth a visit.

### Tripeiros

Porto was where the fleet for Henry the Navigator's assault on Ceuta in 1415 was fitted out. For this Christian venture against the Moors of North Africa, the people of Porto surrendered the finest cuts of meat in their stores to the navy and lived on tripe instead, thus earning the nickname of *Tripeiros* (literally 'tripe eaters').

also houses *Restaurante No Mercado*, a laidback restaurant with an outdoor terrace overlooking the square, where patrons share plates of sizzling tapas – salty padrón peppers, traditional grilled sausage, garlicky chilli-spiked prawns – or delicious wood-fired pizzas.

## PALÁCIO DA BOLSA

The former stock exchange or **Palácio da Bolsa** ❹ (www.palaciodabolsa.com; April–Oct 9am–6.30pm, Nov–March 9am–1pm & 2–5.30pm, guided tours only, 30min), dominating the west side of the square, is a nod to Porto's economic power and prosperity in the late nineteenth century. It was built on the ruins of the ancient convent of São Francisco, which was destroyed by fire, and it remained the city's stock exchange (Bolsa) until the 1990s when it linked up with Lisbon's Bolsa. The desks and benches are long gone, and it has more the feel of a royal residence than a stock exchange. Rooms centre around the glass-domed Pátio das Nações – the former trading floor – decorated with the coats of arms of nations that traded with Portugal. The Noble Stairway leads up to grand chambers such as the Court Room, the Golden Room, the Presidents' Room and the General Assembly Room, culminating with the architectural showstopper: the **Arabian Hall**. Replacing the ballroom and inspired by the Alhambra in Granada, this oval room is adorned with rich Moorish decoration of arabesques and carved woodwork. The room took eighteen years to complete and was embellished with 20 kilos of gold leaf. If you have deep pockets and happen to be looking for a venue, it's available to rent. For those with tighter purse strings, settle for dinner in the on-site restaurant, *O Comercial*, which has an affordable set lunch menu and large windows framing river views.

After lunch, dive headfirst into the bounty of the region's grapes at the **Wines of Portugal Tasting Rooms** (Rua das Flores 8–12; Mon–Sat 11am–7pm; www.winesofportugal.com), a five-minute walk north from the Palácio. It's a very relaxed sort of place, where you can work your way through 28 different wines (or perhaps just cherry-pick a few favourites) in the permanent exhibition. There is English labelling for each bottle, information on wines from different regions, and friendly, helpful staff. Just up the hill the **Douro and Port Wine Institute** (free) is the place to learn about port, with an excellent little museum on how these fortified wines are made and (for a small fee) tastings of different varieties.

## IGREJA DE SÃO FRANCISCO

Beside the Palácio da Bolsa, gazing out over the River Douro, is the imposing **Igreja de São Francisco** ❺ (daily March–May & Oct 9am–7pm; June 9am–7.30pm; July–Sept 9am–8pm; Nov–Feb 9am–6pm). The exterior is simple, grey and Gothic, built as part of

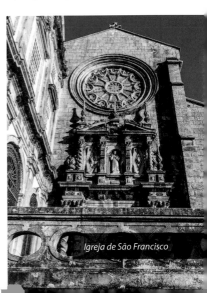

*Igreja de São Francisco*

a Franciscan convent in 1383–1425. But the church's interior is like an explosion in a gold factory, swathed from floor to ceiling with a dazzling riot of gilded rococo woodcarving. The 210kg of gold leaf used for the embellishment of the church came from Brazil, Portugal's former colony. The highlight is the painted altarpiece representing the **Tree of Jesse** (1718–21) on the north wall, depicting Christ's genealogy, the tree rising from the recumbent body of Jesse of Bethlehem, father of King David and culminating in Christ, with Mary and Joseph either side.

The museum displays religious artwork, but of more interest to most visitors are the catacombs. The rich and poor of Porto alike were once buried here, with an estimated 30,000 skulls interred in the cellars. There are numbered panels with dates from 1746–1866 (after which the state banned burials in churches), among them the remains of monks who lived here.

# THE SÉ AND AROUND

The Sé, or Cathedral, is one of the few Romanesque monuments in the city, though much modified since its original construction. It is set high up on the Penaventosa hill and is an unmistakable city landmark. The spacious esplanade, with great views of the old town, tends to attract more crowds than the Sé itself, whose facade is rather austere. It was here that Don João I married Philippa of Lancaster in 1387 and where Henry the Navigator, their fourth son, was baptized in 1394. The quarter around and below the Sé is the oldest in the city and well worth exploring for its warren of steep alleys and stairways. Steps from here lead all the way down to the Ribeira.

## THE SÉ

Built as a Romanesque fortress church with battlements, the **Sé** ❻ (daily April–Oct 9am–6.30pm, Nov–March until 6pm; free, but charge for cloister) is a jigsaw of architectural styles, from Romanesque through Gothic to Baroque. As you step inside the church the eye is inevitably drawn to the monumental altar, flanked by barley twist columns and etched with elaborate gilt carvings of saints and angels. This was the work of Nasoni (see page 47), who in his flamboyant style also decorated the walls of the chancel, embellished the chapels and added the loggia on the north side. In the left transept the Chapel of the Holy Sacrament is bejewelled with an ornate silver retable, executed by local silver-smiths in the seventeenth century in Mannerist style.

Close to the cathedral portal is the entrance to the Cistercian **Cloister**, whose double-tier Corinthian capitals support soaring Gothic arches. The sober granite is accented by seven panels of decorative *azulejos* (tiles) emblazoned with scenes from Solomon's

*Porto's landmark Sé*

*Song of Songs*. A stairway designed by Nasoni, leading to the upper storey, is splashed with eighteenth-century *azulejos* depicting rural and mythological scenes. The adjoining Sala Capitular (Chapter Room) has yet more *azulejos*, this time showing hunting scenes. Steps then take you down to the Treasury, which is a magpie's nest of lavish gold and silver vestments and reliquaries.

## TERREIRO DA SÉ

The spacious square in front of the church, the **Terreiro da Sé** ❼, has a Manueline-style pillory, complete with hooks where criminals were hanged. This is a replica, erected here in 1945, but acts as a solemn nod to the harsh penalties of former times. On the north side of the church is an equestrian statue of a very upright Vímara Peres, vassal of Afonso III of Léon, Count of Portugal, who captured ancient Portucale from the Moors in AD 868. The portico on this side of the church is adorned with fine eighteenth-century *azulejos*. The reconstructed medieval tower just below the esplanade houses one of the city's main tourist offices – with very helpful staff.

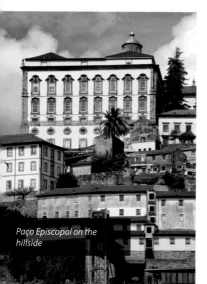

*Paço Episcopal on the hillside*

## PAÇO EPISCOPAL

Abutting the cathedral on the south side of the square is the monumental **Paço Episcopal** ❽ (Bishop's Palace; Mon–Sat 9am–1pm & 2–6pm; guided tours every half-hour), former residence of the bishops of Porto. It was built on the foundation of a former castle but was largely reconstructed by visionary Nasoni in the eighteenth century. The palace has been host to important historical events, including the coronation of the first King of Portugal, as well as serving as a fortress – occupied by the Liberalists – during the Portuguese Civil War, when it was put under siege. It later played a similar role for troops of Sir Arthur Wellesley (later Duke of Wellington) during the Peninsular War. After the fall of the monarchy, it began a new chapter of its life as Porto's city hall and was opened to the public by request under the will of the last bishop.

The palace is a familiar landmark in the city, its four-storey riverside facade one of the most prominent buildings on the hill above Ribeira. A tour of the rooms can be quite heavy-going, particularly trawling through the portraits of all the bishops in the Audience Room, but there are lovely views of the red-roofed jumble and river from the terraces. The architectural highlight is Nasoni's magnificent Baroque main staircase embellished with rococo decorative features; the colourfully decorated glass dome illuminates the whole of the entrance vestibule and stairway.

## CASA-MUSEU GUERRA JUNQUEIRO

Behind the Sé lies the **Casa-Museu Guerra Junqueiro 9** (Tues–Sun 10am–12.30pm & 2–5.30pm; free at weekends), a handsome Baroque mansion tucked away down the charming Rua de Dom Hugo. This was the last home of poet Guerra Junqueiro (1850–1923), who was also a politician, viticulturist, scientist, philosopher and art collector. His works of art are displayed throughout the house, much as they might have been during his lifetime. The collection consists of decorative arts from the fifteenth to nineteenth centuries, including elaborate furniture, fine silver and sculptures, both from Iberia and far-flung corners of the Portuguese empire. A

*Casa-Museu Guerra Junqueiro*

modern section of the museum hosts temporary exhibitions, and there is a tranquil café with outdoor tables overlooking the garden with its statue of the seated poet.

Continue along the Rua Dom Hugo for the restored and remodelled seventeenth-century Capela de Nossa Senhora das Verdades (Tues–Sun 10am–5.30pm, brief closing at lunchtime), a pretty chapel which reopened in 2018 and serves as a welcome centre for pilgrims on their way to Santiago de Compostela. Just beyond, a steep stairway – carved through the remaining sections of the medieval town walls – wends down through the tangle of steep medieval alleys and stairways of the **Barredo** working-class quarter and on to the waterfront.

## IGREJA DE SANTA CLARA

Tucked away on a pretty shaded square, east of the Sé, is the **Igreja de Santa Clara** ❿ (Largo de 1 Dezembro; Mon, Wed–Fri & Sun

9am–12.30pm & 2–5.30pm, Tues & Sat 9am–12.30pm & 2–4.30pm). The squat facade of this inconspicuous church belies a treasure trove of Baroque detail within. The church is of Gothic origin but, like so many churches in Porto, underwent major modifications in the seventeenth and eighteenth centuries. The interior is amazingly lavish, encrusted with gilded Baroque and rococo woodwork *(talhas douradas)*. Almost every inch is cloaked in gold leaf; a spectacular sight when the sun pours in through the windows of the nave. The only unadorned side is the big grill at the back of the church, which shielded the nuns from the convent when they participated in services. Sadly, the convent cloisters are out of bounds, as they are now swallowed up by the neighbouring police station.

The church huddles up to one of the best-preserved parts of the fourteenth-century city wall, the **Murahla Fernandina**, named after King Fernando I. These granite walls at one time surrounded the entire city.

## BAIXA (DOWNTOWN)

The city, which began down by the river, has mushroomed considerably beyond the old walls. The Praça da Liberdade (Freedom Square), at the southern end of Avenida dos Aliados, is regarded as the true heart of the city. To the east of Aliados (as it is commonly called) are the principal shopping streets and the centuries-old Bolhão market, which has been closed for restoration but should reopen in 2022 (a temporary replacement can be found nearby on Rua Fernandes Tomás). The area to the west has undergone a renaissance in the past few years and the quarter around Rua Galeria de Paris and Rua Cândido dos Reis, known jointly as 'the galleries of Paris', buzzes with nightclubs, jazz venues and bars. The Clérigos complex is the main cultural attraction of the Baixa and its lofty tower is a Baroque beacon visible from almost the entire city.

## AVENIDA DOS ALIADOS

Atypical of Porto, the Avenida dos Aliados is a showcase of early twentieth-century Beaux-Arts and neoclassical grandeur. Buildings topped with domes, spires or statues are home to banks, insurance offices and hotels. At the northern end stands the dominant Câmara Municipal (Town Hall), with the neighbouring main tourist office at 25, Rua Clube dos Fenianos. The boulevard slips down to the **Praça da Liberdade ⓫**, a stage for celebrations, festivities, music, merrymaking, mourning and rebellion. At its centre is an equestrian statue of Pedro IV (1798–1834), founder and first ruler of Brazil, who was nicknamed 'The Liberator'. Peering out at the square on the south side, the five-star *InterContinental Hotel* occupies the majestic Palácio das Cardosas. A monastery once stood here but it fell into disrepair and was converted into a private

Estação de São Bento is covered in around 20,000 azulejos

palace in the nineteenth century. The purchase came with one condition: the building would have the same facade that the monks had planned for the reconstruction of the monastery – hence the huge neoclassical exterior. Step inside and it's anything but monastic: all glossy marble, chandeliers and grandeur.

## ESTAÇÃO DE SÃO BENTO

Just east of the square is the ornate **Estação de São Bento** ⑫, far too handsome to be a railway hub. Named after the Benedictine monastery that originally occupied the site, the station was designed by architect José Marquês da Silva and opened in 1916 in the French Beaux-Arts style. Its great entrance hall is plastered with around 20,000 *azulejo* tiles in dazzling cobalt tones. Executed by Jorge Colaço in 1905–16, the decorative panels depict key historical events and scenes of traditional life in Portugal.

## PRAÇA DA BATALHA

Just up Rua 31 de Janeiro from the railway station is the Praça da Batalha with the **Teatro Nacional São João** ⑬ (www.tnsj.pt; guided tours Tues–Sat at 12.30pm; free for children under 10), the city's main theatre and opera venue. Built to replace the late eighteenth-century theatre that was ravaged in a fire, it was designed by architect Marquês da Silva and inspired by the Palais Garnier opera house in Paris. Theatrical productions are usually in Portuguese, but there are tours in English of the splendid auditorium, as well as the rehearsal and dressing rooms.

Conspicuous for its lofty setting above the square is the Baroque **Igreja de São Ildefonso** (Tues–Sun 10am–10.40pm), cloaked with 11,000 *azulejos* depicting scenes from the life of the church's patron saint. The tiles, only added in the early 1930s, were the work of Jorge Colaço, unsurprisingly the same artist who embellished São Bento station.

## RUA DE SANTA CATARINA

Running north from the Igreja de São Ildefonso is the mainly pedestrianized **Rua de Santa Caterina**, the city's main shopping artery. Even for non-shoppers it's an attractive street for a stroll, with mosaic-patterned pavements and an eyeful of glorious facades, from striking Art Nouveau to the flamboyant pink pipes of the Via Catarina shopping mall. Visitors normally make a beeline for the famous **Café Majestic** ⑭ (see page 111) at No. 112, which has been serving coffee since 1921. Originally called the 'Elite', it was known in its earlier life as a meeting place for the political and

---

### A FEAST FOR THE EYES

Apart from one or two captions, some too high to read, there is no information at São Bento station on its hall of *azulejos* – perhaps not surprisingly given this is a station not an art gallery. So, in brief: the dramatic upper panel on the left-hand wall is a scene from the Battle of Arcos de Valdevez, considered Portugal's first War of Independence (1140), when knights led by Afonso I of Portugal fought and defeated troops led by Alfonso VII, King of León. The lower panel shows Egas Moniz offering himself and his wife and sons to the King of León for execution in order to save the besieged town from occupation. The upper panel of the far right-hand wall illustrates the celebratory entrance into Porto in 1387 of King João I of Portugal with his English bride Philippa of Lancaster, daughter of John of Gaunt, thus sealing the long-standing alliance between Portugal and England. The lower panel shows the conquest of the Moors at Ceuta in 1415 led by Henry the Navigator. Other more tranquil scenes portray workers in the vineyards, at the watermill, and, opposite the entrance, Our Lady of the Remedies performing miracles at the holy fountain in the town of Lamego.

cultural set. Today it caters almost entirely to tourists, and prices are sky-high for Porto, but you won't find a more elegant café setting in the city. Further up the street and quite unexpected is the lovely **Capela de Santa Catarina** (confusingly also called the Capela das Almas), completely clad in blue-and-white *azulejos*. The tiles depict scenes from the life of St Francis of Assisi and St Catherine. As is normal with churches in Porto,

*Igreja de São Ildefonso*

the tiles came much later than the church, in this case in 1929, over 130 years after the building was constructed. This is a popular little church and if you visit during Mass, the pews will be packed with worshippers.

## MERCADO DO BOLHÃO

Just west of the Rua de Santa Catarina, you'll find the iconic **Mercado do Bolhão** ⓑ, which has been closed for a complete overhaul but is anticipated to reopen in 2022. The site has hosted a market since 1838 when the city council built a square on a stream-threaded meadow (the name Bolhão means 'big bubble'). The present two-tiered, wrought-iron hall was not built until 1914. For years this has been the belly of the city, with local traders hollering from behind huge piles of fruit and vegetables, and stalls selling live rabbits, tripe, pigs' trotters and all manner of sausages and cheeses. The building has been deteriorating for some

### Um cimbalino

If it's time for a shot of caffeine and you want to sound like a local, ask for a *cimbalino* – an espresso.

time, leading to its closure in 2018 for a hefty refresh. Given the final proposals to use the upper level for shops and restaurants, whether the marketplace clings on to its traditional character remains to be seen.

The area, however, is still an epicurean enclave, with plenty of gourmet temptations around the market square and most of the original stalls temporarily shifted to La Vie shopping centre on nearby Rua Fernandes Tomás. Traditional grocery store *A Pérola do Bolhão*, hidden behind a pastel-yellow Art Nouveau facade on Rua Formosa, is packed with spicy sausages, mountain cheeses, nuts and port wine. On the same street, opposite the market, bakery-grocers' hybrid *Confeitaria do Bolhão* (www.confeitariadobolhao. com) has been serving home-made bread and pastries since 1896; buy baked treats to go or visit the restaurant at lunchtime for the wallet-friendly daily set menu.

## THE CLÉRIGOS COMPLEX

West of Praça da Liberdade, Rua dos Clérigos leads up to the Clérigos Church with its exuberant facade. The Brotherhood of the Clerics (Clérigos), founded in 1707, was a merger of three different brotherhoods in Porto, but all with the same mission – to help members of the clergy in sickness, poverty and death. In 1732–9 the Church of Clérigos was designed by Nicolau Nasoni, the Italian-born architect and painter (see page 47). The brotherhood moved here in 1748.

The 75m-high **Torre dos Clérigos** 🔟 (www.torredosclerigos. pt; daily 9am–7pm; combined ticket available online for church, tower and museum; church only is free), also by Nasoni, was built in 1753 as a landmark for ships navigating the Douro. A climb up the 225 steps is rewarded with unrivalled panoramas of the city (be prepared for queues). Exhibitions and viewing platforms en route allow you to catch your breath, while plaques help you to spot city landmarks and compare the height of other 'skyscrapers in the world'.

From the tower, you can pass through to a museum on the Brotherhood of the Clerics and then continue to the Upper Choir, where dramatic views open up across the beautiful Baroque **Igreja dos Clérigos**, distinguished by its elliptical nave and altarpiece. It was Nasoni's dying wish to be buried here, but no one knows exactly where, or even if he did end up here. Tests are currently being carried out on skeletons discovered during renovations in the hope of solving the mystery.

*Bigger fish to fry at Mercado do Bolhão's fresh food stalls*

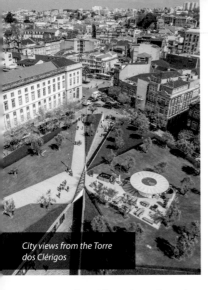

City views from the Torre dos Clérigos

In the lee of the tower is the **Passeio dos Clérigos**, a small modern shopping centre and, more appealing, its landscaped rooftop garden with a chic alfresco bar for coffee, cocktails and lounging on comfy cushions. The olive trees planted here came from the Algarve. Just to the west is the **Jardim da Cordoaria**, in Campo dos Mártires da Pátria, named after the ropemakers *(cordoaria)* who once worked here. Today it's popular with students from the neighbouring university building. The most eye-catching features here are the four sculptures – *Thirteen Laughing at Each Other* – by Spanish artist Juan Muñoz.

## LIVRARIA LELLO

A short stroll up the Rua das Carmelitas brings you to the neo-Gothic facade of the Livraria Chardron, better known as the **Livraria Lello** ⑰ (www.livrarialello.pt; daily 9am–7pm). It's so popular that you have to either book tickets online or purchase a voucher (redeemable against the purchase of books) at the corner shop up the road, where there is invariably a queue. It may seem strange for a bookshop to have an admission fee, but the system was introduced a few years ago when the shop was facing a crisis in the growth of visitor numbers. It's not just the stunning Art Nouveau interior with its dramatic double red staircase and opulent ceiling, nor the wonderful collection of books, old and new, that draw the long queues of punters. It's also the fact that the shop was frequented by *Harry Potter* author J.K. Rowling when she lived and worked as a teacher in Porto in the 1990s (she was married briefly to a Portuguese man) and the bookstore may well have been the inspiration for scenes in Hogwarts.

If you spot young Portuguese in black capes in the city, they are not *Harry Potter* fans but students of Porto University. You may see them coming and going from the huge rectangular university building overlooking the nearby **Praça de Gomes Teixeira**

## NICOLAU NASONI

Nicolau Nasoni was an Italian artist and architect born in Tuscany in 1691. He first worked as an apprentice in Siena before leaving for Malta in 1722, where he painted frescoes in Valletta's cathedral and embellished grand buildings for the Order of the Knights of St John. Porto was thriving in the 1920s and Nasoni moved here in 1925, making it his home. The Portuguese loved his flair for theatrics and he became one of the most influential figures in Portuguese Baroque and rococo architecture, creating, remodelling or enhancing churches and palaces. Nasoni's speciality was an architectural form called *talha dourada* – carved woodwork decorated with gold leaf, producing a flamboyant and opulent effect. He renovated and redecorated Porto's cathedral but his real tour de force was the Clérigos complex (see page 44), which he worked on for over three decades. The prolific architect's work took him beyond Porto and included the Mateus Palace, familiar from the labels on bottles of Mateus Rosé. His final request was to be buried in the Clérigos church, but no one knows where his body rests. Researchers are currently testing skeletal remains found on site to see if his dying wish was honoured.

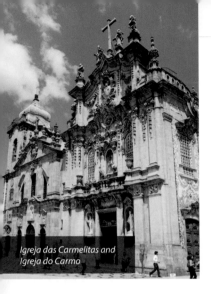

*Igreja das Carmelitas and Igreja do Carmo*

⓲, with its palms and lion fountain. The *Café D'Ouro* on the far side dates back to 1909 and, confusingly, is universally known as **Café Piolho** (www.cafepiolho. com). A meeting place for students and teachers from the university, it is one of most famous cafés in Porto. The two nearby Baroque churches, **Igreja das Carmelitas** and **Igreja do Carmo**, appear at first glance to stand side by side, but look closer and you will see they are separated by a very narrow structure – the thinnest house in Porto. This was built to comply with an unwritten law forbidding two churches to share a common wall, and in this case perhaps ensuring no amorous links between the nuns of the Carmelite Church and the monks of the Carmo church. The east wall of the latter church is decorated by striking blue-and-white *azulejos*, depicting the legendary founding of the Carmelite order on Mount Carmel.

## CENTRO PORTUGUÊS DE FOTOGRAFIA

A stone's throw south of the Clérigos complex, the vast neoclassical building on Largo Amor de Perdição is home to the **Centro Português de Fotografia** ⓳ (Portuguese Centre for Photography; March–June, Sept & Oct Tues–Fri 10am–6pm, Sat & Sun 3–7pm; July & Aug daily 10am–6pm; Nov–Feb Tues–Fri 10am–12.30pm & 2–5pm, Sat & Sun 3–7pm; free). A former prison, it was built in 1767 and housed inmates on three floors: the dark, dank and chilly ground-floor dungeons; the second floor, which was slightly more salubrious and included cells for women; and the third floor with individual prison cells for 'people with status', which were only locked at night. One of the top-floor cells (with some of the finest views of the city) belonged to the famous nineteenth-century novelist, Camilo Castelo Branco, who was locked up here for adultery. A bronze statue in the square outside shows him embracing his naked lover.

The prison was closed in 1974, soon after the Revolution. The building today hosts temporary photography exhibitions and houses a permanent and rare collection of cameras, including nineteenth-century studio cameras used to take pictures for the identification of prisoners and spy cameras from the 60s–80s, disguised as Pepsi cans or Camel cigarette packets.

*Centro Português de Fotografia*

The area to the south was the centre of the medieval **Jewish quarter**. Stroll down the Rua de São Bento da Vitória with the eponymous monastery on the right (guided tours Mon–Fri at noon), built in the seventeenth and eighteenth centuries by Benedictine monks and preserving a beautiful cloister. The road brings you down to the Church of Nossa Senhora da Vitória and the **Miradouro da Vitória ⑳**, with splendid views of Porto and Vila Nova de Gaia across the river. It's a favourite spot at sunset.

## RUA DAS FLORES

To the east, and linking the town centre with Ribeira, is the delightful **Rua das Flores**, or Street of Flowers. The name dates back to the sixteenth century when this was a pocket of gardens belonging to the bishop of Porto. It was favoured by the nobles and bourgeoisie, who built their luxury mansions here. In the nineteenth century the street was the haunt of the literati, and in 1855 a poetry journal was founded here by the 'Poets of the Flores Street Movement'. Only a decade ago this corner of Porto was off the tourist trail: dark and traffic-ridden, with buildings in a state of disrepair. Now pedestrianized and flanked by handsome mansions, seductive shops and cafés, it is a top spot in the city for a leisurely stroll.

At the far end, just before the Largo de São Domingos, you're unlikely to miss the elaborate Baroque facade of the Igreja da Misericórdia by Nicolau Nasoni. Entrance is only possible via the adjoining **Museu da Igreja Misericórdia ㉑** (www.mmipo.pt; daily Oct–March 10am–5.30pm, April–Sept 10am–6.30pm; guided tours available). Until 2013 the building was home to the Santa Casa da Misericórdia, founded in 1499 as a charitable institution providing health care and assisting impoverished prisoners. In 2014 the building underwent a complete transformation, and it is now an interesting little museum. Visits start on the top floor, with a collection of fascinating medical equipment used for brain surgery, electric shock therapy, blood-letting and other largely defunct surgical procedures. The range of exhibits and memorabilia gives a real insight into the breadth of the organization and the help that it gave; its importance to the community is also evidenced by the gallery of solemn portraits of its benefactors. The next floor down displays a range of painting and sculpture from the sixteenth to the eighteenth centuries, and a room of religious artefacts collected by the Misericórdia, including gold and silverware, vestments and tiny crucifixes. The star work of art is on the first floor: the beautiful, enigmatic and anonymous painting, *Fons Vitae* or *The Fountain of Life* (*c*.1520), portraying King Manuel, his wife and his two children on their knees, facing the crucified Christ. Visits end with serene views down into the Misericórdia church.

*Rua das Flores*

# MIRAGAIA AND MASSARELOS

The quarters of Miragaia and Massarelos lie west of the city centre, both bordering the River Douro. Miragaia is one of the most picturesque neighbourhoods of Porto, with its cobbled alleys and jumble of pastel-washed, red-tiled houses climbing the steep slopes. At its eastern end it blends seamlessly with neighbouring Ribeira – marked only by a sudden swell of tourists. The Miragaia district dates back to medieval days when it was outside the city walls, and home to Jews and Armenians. Massarelos, stretching west to the Arrábida Bridge and north up the hillsides towards Boavista, is a larger and more varied quarter. Many of its grander former residences are now part of the university. The main focus for tourists is the **Jardim do Palácio de Cristal**, whose romantic gardens tumble down the hillside and afford glorious river views. This botanical retreat is also home to Almeida Garrett Municipal Library and the Galeria Municipal do Porto, which host regular cultural events and contemporary art exhibitions, respectively.

## RIVERSIDE MIRAGAIA

Miragaia used to be a quarter of fishermen, and the **Igreja de São Pedro de Miragaia** (Tues–Sat 3.30–7pm, Sun 10–11.30am; free) is dedicated to St Peter, patron saint of fishermen. The original medieval church was demolished to make way for this Baroque beauty, and the blue-and-white *azulejos* (tiles) embellishing its facade were added in 1863–76. Inside are gilded wood carvings and, unusually, a sixteenth-century Flemish Pentecost triptych in the Confraria Museum. (If locked, ask nicely and the custodian will usually let you peek inside.)

Miragaia means 'Looking at Gaia', and the views across the river are one of its main attractions. However, some of the best vistas from lower Miragaia were obliterated by the monumental neoclassical **Alfândega Nova** ㉒ (New Customs House), built on the waterfront in 1860–80. Although essential to Porto's burgeoning commerce, it also wiped out the ancient fishermen's beach and a shipyard. The building lost its role when the port moved to Leixões in Matosinhos, but after a modern renovation, it has a new lease of life as a venue for corporate conventions, exhibitions and training programmes.

It is home to the **Museu dos Transportes e Comunicações** (Museum of Transport and Communications; www.amtc.pt; Tues–Fri 10am–1pm & 2–6pm, Sat & Sun 3–7pm, last entry one hour before closing; Customs House Museum is free), accessed at the back of the building. Head up to the first floor for The Engine of the Republic, a display of cars which have served Portugal's presidents since the creation of the Republic In 1910, starting with

*A tableau at World of Discoveries*

a horse-drawn carriage. Comunicar, on the same floor, is a lively multimedia exhibition on the many forms of manmade communication. On the second floor, the rarely visited and antiquated Customs House Museum has no English information apart from a video on the history of the building.

If you have children in tow, they are more likely to be enthralled by the **World of Discoveries** (www.worldofdiscoveries.com; Tues–Fri 10am–6pm, Sat & Sun 10am–7pm, last entry half-hour before closing) behind the Alfândega Nova, a theme park and interactive museum on Portugal's history. It's all good fun and an easy way for youngsters to learn about the great Portuguese explorers, the lands they discovered and the caravels they sailed in. The grand finale is the Disney-style boat trip, with audioguides, through 'the New Worlds'.

*Museu Nacional de Soares dos Reis*

# MUSEU NACIONAL DE SOARES DOS REIS

The northern tip of Miragaia flaunts one of Porto's largest and most imposing palaces, which now houses the **Museu Nacional de Soares dos Reis ㉓** (Rua de Dom Manuel ll 44; www.museu-soaresdosreis.gov.pt; Tues–Sun 10am–5.30pm), the main art gallery of Porto. The neoclassical Carrancas palace was once home to the Jewish family of Moraes e Castro, nicknamed Carranca, who operated a flourishing gold and silver workshop here. The French General and Statesman, Marshal Soult, lived here for six weeks in 1809 during the Peninsular War, before being driven out by troops under the command of Arthur Wellesley (the future Duke of Wellington). The palace has also been the abode of royalty. Founded in 1933, the museum was created as a repository for works of art taken from convents that had been abandoned or abolished during the Portuguese Civil War. The museum wraps around a delightful courtyard and a garden of camellia trees, with *azulejos* and a garden-view café.

The permanent collection starts on the second floor with the decorative arts: fine porcelain, silver, glass and furnishings. Highlights include a large tapestry depicting the return of Vasco da Gama from the east and some small French and Flemish paintings, among them a keenly observed portrait of a woman by Clouet, the sixteenth-century court painter of Henry II of France. The more modern galleries on the first floor are hung with paintings from the nineteenth to the twentieth centuries, notable among them the landscapes of Silva Porto and the Impressionist-style paintings of Italy and Portugal by Henrique Pousão, who died in 1884 at the age of 25.

But the highlight of the museum is the gallery devoted to works by nineteenth-century sculptor António Soares dos Reis. Born in 1847 in Vila Nova da Gaia – which was also where he died by suicide at the age of 41 – he was greatly influenced by his stays in

Paris and Rome, where he learned to work with Carrara marble, famously used by Michelangelo. Although largely unrecognized during his lifetime, he was prolific and versatile, producing works in plaster, bronze and marble, portraying historical, allegorical and contemporary figures. Particularly moving are the *Bust of the Negro Boy*, *Youth with the Hammer* and what is widely held as his finest work, the classical *O Desterrado* (*The Exile*), executed when he was only 24. There are also realistic busts of contemporaries and grandees.

## THE ARTS BLOCK

Straddling the northern border of Miragaia is the **Rua de Miguel Bombarda**, the beating cultural heart of Porto. The city's artistic renaissance took root in Bombarda – the neighbourhood named

The Annunciation *at the Museu Nacional de Soares dos Reis*

for this *rua* – when a scattering of independent art galleries sprung up along the street during the depths of the economic crisis. A couple of the best include Cruzes Canhoto (at No.452) and Ó! Galería (No.61). Today, the district brims with private galleries, cool concept stores, vintage shops and design boutiques. Every two months the galleries simultaneously hold exciting exhibitions by homegrown and international artists, normally on a Saturday from 4–5pm. Entry to the galleries is free. At Rua Miguel Bombarda 285 is the misleadingly named **Centro Comercial Bombarda** ㉔ (CCB; Mon–Sat noon–8pm), a small and sleek shopping centre and creative hub of independent Portuguese boutiques and galleries. Novelty is the byword here: a stucco ear perhaps, a papier mâché head (and you can watch them being made), a knitted bow tie, organic cosmetics, vintage accessories, edgy jewellery and a sustainable minifarm selling organic goods. If you're visiting the quarter, note that the opening hours are normally Monday to Saturday from noon until 7pm.

## JARDINS DO PALÁCIO DE CRISTAL

Bordering Miragaia in Massarelos is the 20-acre **Jardins do Palácio de Cristal** ㉕ (main entrance Rua Dom Manuel II; daily 8am–9pm; free at weekends), sculpted hillside gardens that offer some of the best river views in the city. From the south side you can even spot the Atlantic rollers at Foz do Douro. A natural magnet for city-dwellers, this green lung of the city has exotic trees and plants, themed gardens, fountains, ponds and statues – not to mention the strutting peacocks and noisy cockerels who roam freely in this leafy haven.

The garden was originally designed in the nineteenth century by German landscape architect Émille David. The **Palácio de Cristal** (daily April–Sept 8am–9pm, Oct–March 8am–7pm; free), a mushroom-like domed sports arena, was built in 1951 for the

World Hockey Championships. It replaced a rather more elegant iron and glass palace, similar to London's Crystal Palace, dating from the 1860s. The building is also called the Pavilhão Rosa Mota, after the Portuguese Olympic marathon champion. With a seating capacity of 10,000, the pavilion holds concerts and sporting events and is one of Porto's leading entertainment venues.

Set in the green splendour of the gardens to the west is the **Museu Romântico** ❷ (Tues–Sun 10am–5.30pm). The house was bought in the early nineteenth century by a port wine millionaire, Antonio Ferreira Pinto Basto, but its main claim to fame is as the last home of Carlos Alberto, the King of Piedmont and Sardinia – albeit he only lived here for a couple of months before dying in 1849. The previous year he had led one of the Liberation movements in the Unification of Italy, but was defeated by the

*Jardins do Palácio de Cristal*

Austrians in the Battle of Novar in 1849 and abdicated in favour of his eldest son, Victor Emmanuel, before fleeing to Portugal. Pinto Basto offered him refuge in his mansion in Porto. The house was bought by the state in the mid-twentieth century and opened as the Museum of Quinta da Macieirinha in 1972. It is laid out more or less as it would have been in the king's day, peppered with his works of art and furniture; some original, some reproductions. A visit takes in various salons, the oratory where the king attended mass daily, the Ball Room and the King's Hall where he received visitors and where his body lay in state.

Next to the museum is *Antiqvvm* (see page 112), a swish restaurant with Michelin-starred cuisine and a garden terrace offering breathtaking river views. But beware: deep pockets are essential – and you probably need to book in advance.

Steps from the museum lead all the way down to the riverfront, passing the Baroque **Igreja de Massarelos** en route, with its bell towers and tiled facade. The church was built on the site of a ruined chapel founded in 1394 by the Brotherhood of the Amas do Corpo Santo, a group of navigators who had survived a storm when returning from England. The brotherhood was dedicated to the protection of seafarers and merchants, and it is rumoured that Henry the Navigator was a member.

## ALONG THE WATERFRONT

On the riverfront going west is the **Museu do Carro Eléctrico** ㉗ (Tram Museum; www.museudocarroelectrico.pt; Mon 2–6pm, Tues–Sun 10am–1pm & 2–6pm), a fascinating insight into the evolution of the tram network in Porto. Better still, you can actually hop on a working vintage tram; both #18 and #1 stop here – the latter is particularly scenic, running beside the river from central Porto to Foz do Douro on the coast. The large letters on the museum building, STCP, stand for the Sociedade de Transportes

Coletivos do Porto. The organization resurrected a couple of tram routes in the city and opened a museum in 1992 in the Massarelos thermoelectric power plant, which fed the network for the first 45 years. The century-old machines have been restored and are now on view in the Machinery Hall. The trams on display span over 100 years, from an early horse-drawn tram-car to a special tram for smokers (the *fumista*), tramcars for the transport of fish and familiar models of the late twentieth century.

Scenes westwards to the Atlantic are framed by the vast concrete swoop of the **Ponte da Arrábida** ㉘, curving gracefully above the River Douro. When it opened in 1963 this was the longest concrete arch in the world. There is no pedestrian access across, but should you wish to climb over the bridge check out www.portobridgeclimb.com.

*Museu do Carro Eléctrico*

# BOAVISTA AND SERRALVES

Northwest of the city centre, Boavista is an upmarket enclave of luxury hotels, designer stores, villas and one of the city's top sights: the Casa da Música or House of Music. The Avenida da Boavista slices through suburbia and stretches westwards all the way to the Atlantic coast at Foz do Douro. At the Porto end is the huge roundabout, Praça Mouzinho de Albuquerque, more familiarly known as the Rotunda da Boavista, with a central garden, the Jardim da Boavista. The column at its centre, the Monumento aos Heróis da Guerra Peninsular, commemorates the defeat of the French in the Peninsular War (1807–14). The lion, symbolizing the alliance between the Portuguese and British, is bringing down the Imperial Eagle, carried into battle by the Grande Armée of Napoleon.

Between Boavista and the coast is the outstanding Serralves Museum of Contemporary Art and its beautiful park.

## The Porto Card

The Porto Card includes free admission or reduced fees to museums and tourist attractions, plus an optional travel card for unlimited access to metro, buses and urban trains. Cards are available online (www.visitportoandnorth.travel) and at tourist offices. A card without transport costs €6, €10, €13 and €15 for 1, 2, 3 and 4 days; passes with travel for the same periods are €13, €20, €25 and €33.

## CASA DA MÚSICA

On the northwest side of the Rotunda da Boavista, you are unlikely to miss the space-age **Casa da Música** ㉙ (www.casadamusica.com; guided tours in Portuguese and English at 11am and 4pm), an exuberant, avant-garde concert hall designed by Dutch architect (and *Star Wars* fan) Rem Koolhaas. A driver behind Porto's

*The arresting Casa da Música*

resurgent cultural scene, it hosts world-class concerts that attract large numbers of music fans to the city. Concerts range from pop to Baroque, with DJs some nights and the occasional free (or very cheap) event. The main auditorium seats around 1300 and, unusually, is lit with natural daylight through two walls made entirely of glass. A second auditorium accommodates 300 seated and 600 standing. These can be seen on informative, hour-long guided tours of the seventh-floor building, offering a peek into the likes of the VIP hall and rooftop terrace with fine views. The top-floor *Casa da Música Restaurant*, temporarily closed at the time of writing in 2022, has good-value set menus.

## MARKET, CEMETERY AND SYNAGOGUE

To the south of the Boavista Rotunda (and technically in Massarelos) is the renovated **Mercado de Bom Sucesso** (Praça Bom Sucesso 3; Mon–Thurs & Sun 10am–11pm, Fri & Sat 8am–midnight), which lives up to its name: a whole range of beautifully presented gourmet treats under one stylish roof. Along with fresh produce for sale, there are 44 outlets for quick and tasty meals or tapas, including delis with delicious hams and suckling pig and seafood stalls with squid and ceviche. Just take your pick and choose a table. Tables are warmed by heaters in the winter months. Within the same complex is the four-star *Hotel da Música* where, as you probably guessed, music is the theme.

To the west is the **Cemitério de Agramonte** (Rua de Agramonte; daily 8.30am–4.45pm; free), looking a little out of place in the largely modern surroundings. Built in 1855 for the victims of a plague epidemic, the cemetery was later expanded to accommodate the graves of Porto's literati and well-heeled. A fine collection of sculpture Includes works by Soares dos Reis (see page 55 for the Museu Nacional Soares dos Reis) and António Teixeira Lopes. If the cemetery is shut, you can peek through the metal railings at some of the incredibly elaborate mausoleums.

*Fundação Serralves knows a trick or two*

On the far side of the cemetery, accessed from the Rua Guerra Junqueiro, is the striking Art Deco **Sinagoge Kadoorie** (www.comunidade-israelita-porto.org), the largest synagogue in the Iberian peninsula. For security reasons visits and tours are by appointment only (email: tourism@

comunidade-israelita-porta.org). A guided visit gives a fascinating history of the synagogue, its founder and the story of Jews in Portugal and Spain over 500 years.

## FUNDAÇÃO SERRALVES

Between Boavista and the coast lies an outstanding cultural hub, the **Fundação Serralves** (Rua Dom João de Castro 210; 3.5km from Jardim Boavista, 6km west of the city centre; www.serralves.pt; Mon–Fri 10am–7pm, Sat & Sun 10am–8pm; combined ticket for Museum, Villa and Park, or half-price for park only; whole complex free on first Sun of month). From Casa da Música metro station you can take buses #201, #203, #502 or #504.

The complex is most famously home to the **Museu de Arte Contemporânea** ③⓪ (Museum of Contemporary Art). The most

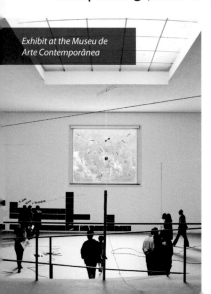

*Exhibit at the Museu de Arte Contemporânea*

influential contemporary art museum in Portugal, it is the brainchild of Álvaro Siza Vieira, 1992 winner of the prestigious Pritzker Prize and one of the world's finest architects. The fourteen exhibition halls are awash with light, and the 4500-strong artworks are striking against vivid white walls. The focus is on art from the 1960s to the present day, with regularly changing exhibitions showcasing the talent of leading local and international artists. Serralves is also a venue

*Ferreira's port wine cellar*

for concerts, dance performances and other events, including the annual art-themed Serralves em Festa, which takes place in May or June. Before you leave, browse the bookstore and gift shop full of creative pieces by Portuguese designers, or have lunch in the peaceful garden restaurant or *casa de chà* (teahouse).

The museum is set in the magnificent 44.5-acre **Serralves Park**, a harmonious series of gardens, tree-lined paths and woodlands, with a lake and even a traditional farm. The grounds are peppered with sculptures and other artworks from the Serralves collection, including a whopping and very photogenic red trowel by Claes Oldenburg. A highlight here is the **Casa de Serralves**, a beautiful pink-hued Art Deco villa from the 1930s, originally designed as a private residence by the second Count of Vizela, Carlos Alberto Cabral. The villa, which occasionally showcases temporary exhibitions, looks stunning against the greenery and is particularly impressive if approached via the fountains.

# VILA NOVA DE GAIA

No trip to Porto is complete without a visit to the cellars of at least one of the port wine lodges where the city's most famous export is stored and aged. These are all located at Vila Nova de Gaia (or just Gaia), across the River Douro and technically a separate city from Porto. The port is actually produced 97km inland in the Upper Douro region, where vines are grown on the steep stone terraces. Here, the blisteringly hot summers and freezing winters create a unique microclimate that produces intensely flavourful grapes. But it's Porto, with its mild and humid climate, that provides the ideal conditions for storing the wines, and every spring the young ports are brought down from river-hugging *quintas* (estates) to the cellars in Vila Gaia de Nova. Until 1987 port could not be called port

*The tasting halls of family-run Taylor's*

unless it was matured here, and this is still very much the hub of the industry.

You can of course taste port all over the city, but the port wine merchants only operate in Gaia and this is where tours, followed by tastings, take place. You can get here simply by crossing on the lower level of the Dom Luís I bridge – alternatively, there are buses from the centre, or you can take the metro to Jardim do Morro and walk down to the waterfront.

> **Cellar visits**
>
> For information on reservations and opening hours of the port wine lodges, visit the website of AEVP, the Association of Port Wine Companies, at www.aevp.pt.

## PORT WINE LODGES

Wine lodges give you the chance to visit barrel-lined cellars, learn how port is made and, over what are normally quite generous tastings, discover how to distinguish the different aromas and flavours. Fifteen port producers are based here, and most of the famous ones have their neon names (many still British) emblazoned above the lodges. The port sold here is the same price as you'll find in shops all over the city, but the advantage is that you can try before you buy. Tastings may be accompanied (usually at extra cost) by olives and salted almonds (good with dry white port), blue cheese and chocolate (with vintage ruby port), and nutty cheese and *foie gras* (with 10-year-old tawny port). After a few tastings you'll soon realize that a bottle of port is not just for Christmas.

Some lodges require bookings, notably *Graham's* (see page 68). For others, reservations are not always essential, but it's still a good idea to call ahead to confirm times. Most tourist maps of Porto don't show the lodges, but the Gaia tourist office on the waterfront has a useful Wine Tourism Guide, with all of them marked. Most are open daily; a few close at lunchtime. Tours and tastings start from about €12, but if you want to taste vintage ports expect to pay a lot more.

The port houses lining the riverfront invariably attract the most tourists. To avoid the crowds and enjoy the best views and most exclusive wine lodges, you need to climb up the hill or take a taxi. Port connoisseurs usually head up the hill to **Graham's** ㉛ (www. grahams-port.com), a sophisticated, late nineteenth-century lodge, with a professional tour, short video, tasting rooms and an excellent restaurant (*Vinum*, see page 113) and shop (anyone for the 1882 vintage at €6,000 a bottle?).

**Taylor's** ㉜ (www.taylor.pt), a walk or short taxi ride up Rua do Choupelo, is another top producer, dating back to 1692 and still family-run. Here you can take a fairly extensive and very informative self-guided audio tour (no booking necessary) with films,

## A PORT ENTREPRENEUR

Against all the odds in a male-dominated sector, Antónia Ferreira (1811–96), affectionately known as 'A Ferreirinha' or 'Little Ferreira' (she was only 4ft 11ins tall), became famous for her formidable role in port production and winemaking innovation. She was hugely energetic and ran the Ferreira company from 1844 until her death in 1896. A picture of her hangs in the Ferreira port wine lodge on Avenida de Ramos Pinto, just back from the waterfront. The diminutive port producer was almost drowned when the boat she was on capsized in the rapids of the Douro in 1861, but was saved by her crinoline which kept her afloat – unlike her unfortunate English friend, Baron de Forrester, wine merchant and owner of the boat, who drowned. A stone marks the spot on the river where he died.

exhibits and images, ending with tastings of its Chip Dry (Extra Dry White) and LBV (Late Bottled Vintage), invented in the 1930s and 1970s, respectively. If you're feeling flush, a visit could be preceded or followed by a sumptuous lunch or dinner at Taylor's *Barão Fladgate* restaurant, with fabulous views over Porto and the River Douro. **Churchill's** 33 (www.churchills-port.com), below Graham's, is smaller and more intimate than the

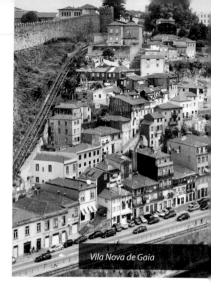
*Vila Nova de Gaia*

other lodges, with cheaper tours. For a Portuguese wine lodge, try **Ferreira** 34 (www.sograpevinhos.com), one of the largest in Gaia and the only major port wine house to have remained in Portuguese hands since its foundation over 250 years ago (see box, opposite).

If time is limited and you want to taste port without a tour, head for the *Sogevinus Wine Shop* on the waterfront (Avenida Ramos Pinto, 280), a port-wine holding company with a good variety of ports and wines from its four brands. Prices are no higher than those you'd find in the port wine cellars. Another option is the very conspicuous **Espaço Porto Cruz** 35 (www.myportocruz.com), a swish four-storey building on the waterfront with tastings on the second floor, a restaurant on the third and a panoramic 360-degree lounge on the fourth. With its comfy cushioned seats, port wines, cocktails and superlative views, this rooftop bar is a great location at sunset.

### Raise a glass: World of Wine

A new museum complex opened its doors in Vila Nova de Gaia in 2020, as part of a mammoth project to transform the city's former wine warehouse district into a cultural quarter. It took five years of renovation works and a cost of €105m (£95m) to launch the World of Wine (WoW), a sprawling dockside hub spread across 55,000sq metres of restored port cellars. Arranged around an open-air square, WoW includes seven museums, five restaurants, shops, bars, event spaces, exhibitions halls and even a wine school offering short courses focusing on Portuguese viticulture and gastronomy. In addition to the temple to wine, the other immersive museums provide an insight into the key industries, from cork to chocolate and textiles, that make up the fabric of the country.

## THE RIVERFRONT

There are other attractions in Gaia apart from port, notably the superb views across to Porto. These can be admired from the quayside or from the terraces of many of the cafés and restaurants. Serious foodies will be heading up the hill to *The Yeatman* (see page 113), Porto's culinary big-hitter with two Michelin stars. But if all you're after is a quick bite, try the reinvented Mercado Beira Rio, just back from the riverfront, where fresh fruit, vegetables and colourful flowers now coexist with some seriously good food stalls.

Moored along the river are replicas of the *barcos rabelos*, the flat-bottomed sailboats that used to bring the new port wine down from the Douro Valley in wooden casks. During the second day of the feast of São João (24 June), the *rabelos* scuttle down the River Douro in colourful races. Today, cruise boats of all descriptions can be seen along the waterfront, including the larger craft at the western end which offer week-long cruises to the Douro Valley.

It is tempting to while away the hours on the waterfront and savour the views across the river, but spare time too for the quaint alleys behind, where you'll find more local life, hole-in-the-wall tavernas and some eye-catching urban art. Rua Cândido dos Reis (going up from Sandeman's cellars) is one of the more character-ful streets. To the east, the pretty Igreja de Santa Marinha, with its slender bell tower, was one of many churches in Porto remodelled by prolific Baroque architect Nicolau Nasoni.

### Vintage port

A bottle of vintage port should be consumed within 48 hours of opening. Whether at home or in Portugal, don't pay a high price for a glass of a rare vintage port unless the bartender or waiter opens the bottle in front of you. For most establishments that's too expensive a proposition.

## MOSTEIRO DA SERRA DO PILAR

The panoramic **Teleférico de Gaia** ③⑥ (cablecar; www.gaiacablecar. com; May–Sept daily 10am–8pm, 6pm off-season) climbs above the riverfront, affording peerless views of Porto and the wine lodges below. In five minutes you are at the **Jardim do Morro** ③⑦, an attractive and well-tended garden with lush lawns, colourful flowerbeds and stone benches where you can sit and take in the views. The gardens can also be accessed up a thigh-crunching flight of steps from the Gaia waterfront. Presiding over Gaia on the hilltop is the **Mosteiro da Serra do Pilar** ③⑧ (Mon–Sat 9am–5pm, later in summer), accessed by crossing the main road (near the metro) followed by a five-minute climb up the hill. The monastery can also be reached from the upper level of the Dom Luís I bridge or via the metro to Jardim do Morro.

*Mosteiro da Serra do Pilar*

Construction of the monastery began in 1538, but due to lack of funding and political turmoil wasn't completed for over 100 years. It is a remarkable building, unique in the Iberian peninsula for its circular floorplan and cloister. Originally occupied by Augustinian Friars, its role in more recent history has been more military than religious. Strategically located over the river, it played a key role in the defence against the Napoleonic invasions. It was from the terrace here that Lord Wellesley, the future Duke of Wellington, planned his surprise attack on the French in 1809. More recently, the Liberals occupied the monastery while defending it against the Absolutists during the Portuguese Civil War (1824–34). The monastery is still a military base, so don't be surprised to see soldiers in army fatigues.

The belvedere affords incredible views of the river and Porto; even more spectacular if you climb the 100-plus steps to the dome on a guided tour, which also covers the church, cloister and an exhibition on World Heritage Sites. For a reduced rate you can visit the peaceful cloister independent of a guide.

## EXCURSIONS

For visitors with time to venture beyond the city, there are plenty of options. The River Douro is by far the biggest attraction, with boat trips ranging from the one-hour Six Bridges tour to a week's cruise to the port-producing upper Douro Valley. Porto is a springboard for this scenic wine-growing region, and from the city it can be reached by rail and road as well as river.

For more local trips, consider crossing the river to the sleepy fishing village of Alfurada or taking a vintage tram to the Atlantic-battered beaches of Foz do Douro. Short city breaks are the norm for Porto, but for those staying longer there is a clutch of historic cities worth considering for a day-trip: Braga, boasting Portugal's most spectacularly sited sanctuary; the historic centre of Guimarães, first capital of Portugal; attractive Amarante, springing up like a pop-up book from a gorge of the River Tâmega; and, to the south of Porto, the charming university city of Coimbra. All are easily reached by train.

## CANTINHO DAS AROMÁTICAS

If you're visiting Porto in spring or summer and want a break from the port tasting, follow your nose to the fragrant fields and nurseries of **Cantinho das Aromáticas** ❸❾ (Rua do Meiral, 508). Draped across a hilltop in Vila Nova de Gaia, this organic farm produces more than 150 plant species. Slopes are combed with neat rows of sweet-scented flowers, medicinal plants and kitchen herbs. While away a pleasant couple of hours wandering through the colourful fields; be sure to peek inside the ancient dovecote too.

## SIX BRIDGES CRUISE

On a sunny day, nothing compares to a languid one-hour cruise along the River Douro, puttering beneath or past the city's six bridges and admiring their remarkable engineering and elegance. Boat tour companies have kiosks on both sides of the river; varying in price (€12–15), and some include a voucher for port-tasting at Vila Nova de Gaia.

English-speaking commentary covers the history of the bridges. First is the iconic Ponte Dom Luís I, which has connected Porto and Vila Nova de Gaia since 1886. It was designed by Théophile Seyrig, former partner of Gustave Eiffel – of Eiffel Tower fame. The photogenic two-tier structure provides a wonderful backdrop for snapshots and looks spectacular illuminated at night. Originally crossed by mule-drawn carriages, it was equipped with tram tracks on the upper deck in 1905 and adapted for the metro in 2003–5.

Pedestrians can cross on either deck and in summer local youngsters can be seen leaping into the river from the lower level (collecting tourist euros for encouragement). Next along is the slender, graceful **Ponte do Infante**: with its 280m arch span, it's the longest of the bridges over the Douro. Built in 2003, it is also the newest.

Eiffel failed in his bid for the Dom Ponte Luís I, but in the 1870s he was commissioned to design the elegant railway bridge to the east, the now disused **Ponte Dona Maria Pia**, named after the then Queen of Portugal. It carried trains across the water until 1991. Plans to reopen it as a pedestrian and cycle way have never materialized. It was superseded by the futuristic **Ponte São João** (1991), which you can see just beyond it. The pillars of the newer bridge are hollow, making space for interior lifts and stairs that enable inspection of the structure. The old bridge has been retained as a monument and is treasured by locals.

The boat will loop back around before reaching the modern **Ponte do Freizo** (1995), but it can be seen curving above the water in the distance. You then head towards the Atlantic, and the final bridge is the **Ponte da Arrábida**. With a span of 270 metres, this was the largest concrete-arch bridge in the world at the time of its inauguration in 1963.

## FOZ DO DOURO AND MATOSINHOS

Only 5km northwest of Porto lies the well-heeled seaside suburb of Foz do Douro (or simply Foz), and just north of it, Matosinhos, an industrial huddle of warehouses and docks laced by a huge sandy beach and backed by an old quarter with excellent fish restaurants. After a day or two of city sightseeing in Porto it's fun to hop on the wood-panelled carriages of vintage tram #1, trundle along the riverside and arrive at the Atlantic shore. From Foz to Matosinhos it's about an hour's walk, but you can always take bus #500 or hop on the metro.

**Foz do Douro** ⓐ means 'Mouth of the River', and this desirable suburb sits where the River Douro empties into the Atlantic. With

## BRIDGE CLIMBING

If you spy little figures on the Ponte da Arrábida, they will be on a guided ascent with the Porto Bridge Climb (www.portobridge-climb.com). Anyone over 12 years with a head for heights can join a (harnessed) climb up 262 steps to the top of the arch for stunning views – with a nerve-quelling shot of port wine at the top. Just beyond the bridge, the river meets the ocean and you can often spot the white horses of the Atlantic in the far distance.

*Jardim do Passeio Alegre*

its elegant houses, palm-strewn gardens, sun-bleached beaches and long waterfront promenade, Foz became a seaside resort in the nineteenth century and was particularly popular with the British – hence the Praia dos Ingleses. The sandy sweeps are fine for chilling out on a deckchair or enjoying the sunset over a cocktail, but remember that this is the Atlantic, with cold water and power-ful waves when it's windy – more popular with surfers than casual bathers. Beware, too, of the rocks that are found on most beaches.

The tram rattles as far as the **Jardim do Passeio Alegre** in Foz, the delightful riverside gardens with lofty palms, ponds, fountains, sculptures and shady benches beneath plane trees. Behind lies Foz Velha, the quaint old town with a tangle of attractive steep, cob-bled streets. Hidden away here is one of the best restaurants in the region, the *Pedro Lemos* (see page 114), which serves Michelin-starred cuisine in a beautifully restored stone house and on its foliage-strewn roof terrace. On the seafront the prominent **Fort of**

**São João da Foz** (Mon–Fri 9am–5pm; free) was built in 1570–1647 to protect the coast and the mouth of the River Douro. There is not much to see inside, but the ramparts and watchtower afford fine views of the coast. These are particularly dramatic on windy days when the Atlantic rollers crash against the lighthouse. A stroll on the promenade takes you alongside a string of sandy and rocky beaches, punctuated with bar terraces for enjoying the ocean views. These are very popular spots at sunset. Above the Praia do Molhe is the elegant 1930s **Pérgola da Foz**, modelled on the pergola of the Promenade des Anglais in Nice.

If you continue north you come to the Praça de Gonçalves Zarco, a large roundabout overlooked by the seventeenth-century Forte de São Francisco Zavier, better known as **Castelo do Queijo** (Cheese Castle; Tues–Sun 9am–6pm), so-called because

*Piscina das Marés, Leça da Palmeira*

*Castelo do Queijo*

of the shape of the rock it sits on. Opposite is **Sea Life Porto**, a large aquarium which is always a hit with youngsters (see page 93), while spreading inland is the vast **Parque da Cidade** (City Park), the green lung of Porto. Sprawling over 83 acres, this is an oasis for urban-dwellers, with an abundance of flora and fauna, small lakes with ducks and geese, bike paths and sports fields.

The huge beach at **Matosinhos** ⓐ, sheltered by the harbour, is a popular spot for learner surfers. A handful of surfing schools offers lessons and rentals, as well as other watersport facilities and equipment. Being so close to Porto and with easy access by metro, the sands get packed in high season.

From the waterfront you can see the gleaming **Terminal de Cruzeiros** (Cruiseship Terminal), a swirling white structure which has scooped awards for architecture and design. Opened in 2015, it was designed by Luís Pedro Silva and has witnessed a surge in cruise ships to Porto. The interior is super-slick, but unless you are a passenger you can only visit on the weekly guided tour (Sun 9.30am–1pm). The evocative sculpture behind the beach, the Tragédia do Mar, honours the victims of the shipwreck of four trawlers in 1947, when 150 fishermen lost their lives.

The excellent modern tourist office by the beach has a use-ful booklet in English on Matosinhos. The port brands itself WBF,

'World's Best Fish', and helpful staff here will point you in the direction of the nearby seafood restaurants and fish market. You'll soon see that day's catch being grilled on barbecues along the Rua dos Heróis de França. Don't go expecting elegant interiors and picturesque sea views. This is an authentic workaday place, formerly full of canned-fish factories (some still survive), and most of the restaurants are family-run, no-frills affairs with chalked-up menus in Portuguese – but that's the beauty of it. You can still eat reasonably cheaply, although with menus appearing in English and a new safety regulation stipulating glassed-in terraces along the street, prices are rising. A whole range of fish and seafood is on offer and helpings are huge; often half portions suffice.

Locals buy fish from the dock opposite the restaurants. You won't see many tourists, but if you're self-catering or want to watch

*Mercado de Matosinhos*

the action there is nothing stopping you joining the locals. You can also see the catch laid out on the lower level of the modern **Mercado de Matosinhos** nearby, although early morning is the best time to go. On the level above are stalls of fresh fruit and veg, along with cages of chickens, cockerels, ducks and rabbits.

## AFURADA

Beyond the Arrábida bridge, close to where the River Douro collides with the Atlantic, you can cross the river to explore the fishing village of **Afurada** ❷ in Vila Nova de Gaia. Hop on the small Flor

---

### LEÇA DA PALMEIRA

Across the harbour from Matosinhos at Leça da Palmeira are two architectural showstoppers. Merging seamlessly with the rocks and secluded on a wooded hill overlooking the sea is the Piscina das Marés (Sea Pool; mid-June to mid-Sept; daily 9am–7pm). The pair of beautiful stone-hewn seawater pools were designed in 1966 by leading Portuguese architect, Álvaro Siza Vieira, a Matosinhos-born Pritzker prize winner best known for the Contemporary Art Museum at Serralves. The Piscina das Marés has a remarkably contemporary feel even though it was designed over 50 years ago. There are two swimming pools: one for adults, one for children. Another design knockout by the same architect, 1.5km (to the north, is the *Casa de Chá da Boa Nova* (Avenida da Liberdade No. 1681). This is not your normal teahouse *(casa de chà)*; in fact, it's a sleek structure built into the rocks above the sea – declared a National Monument, no less, in 2011. You won't be disappointed when you step inside the door either, not when you have Portugal's best-known chef, Rui Paula, at the helm of the kitchen and churning out inventive gourmet creations.

The Douro Valley

de Gás ferry (from Cais do Ouro; 7am–7.30pm every 15–30 mins depending on season). If you arrive at lunchtime, wafts of charcoal-grilled sardines and squid will greet you as you step off the pier. Along the waterfront are fishing boats, trawlers and nets, with gulls screeching overhead for fishy titbits. It's hard to go wrong when it comes to restaurants here. All will serve you fresh fish, whether it's the unassuming *Café Vapor*, the ever-popular, azulejo-clad *Taberna São Pedro* or the latest addition to the foodie scene, *Armezem de Peize*, opposite the market.

As you wander along the seafront, you'll notice lines of washing flapping noisily in the breeze; the concrete building nearby is a communal washhouse where locals still come to do their laundry. They each have their own washing line, and nothing ever gets nicked. There's a low-key interpretive centre with fishing boats and marine memorabilia donated by the villagers, and a swish marina that feels slightly out of place. You can take a bike across on the

*Boat trips along the Douro open up the wine-growing region*

ferry and from Afurada cycle all the way to the beaches of Espinho (most of it by the sea), passing the Douro Estuary Natural Reserve en route (see page 96).

## DOURO VALLEY

About 80km upstream from Porto the River Douro, or Golden River, twists through deep-cleft gorges, terraced with vineyards. Birthplace of port wine, the scenic **Vale do Douro** ㊹ was classified by Unesco as a World Heritage Site in 2001. The schist soil and the climate are ideal for the growing of grapes, which are behind Douro wines and the famous ports. The wine is made here, then after six months it is carted to the cooler climes of Porto to be aged in its cellars. It is only in recent years that the region has opened up to eco-tourism. Some of the *quintas* (wine estates) offer guided tours and tastings, and a few are open for overnight stays. The best times to visit the region, for the colours and climate, are spring and autumn. The Douro Valley is blasted by hot, dry summers and severe winters; locals sum up the climate as 'nine months of winter, three months of hell'!

As a visitor to the Douro Valley, expect a bewildering choice of options. You can visit independently by road, rail or river; combine a mix of river and rail; or, if time is tight, take a single-day guided excursion by minibus, which will include the best of the scenery, a visit to a couple of vineyards and an hour's boat trip on the most scenic part of the river. With time in hand, go for a couple of days, stay at a *quinta* and enjoy the scenery, the culture and the cuisine at leisure.

A day's boat trip might seem the most appealing option, but beware that the craft are very crowded in season and the limited seats on the upper deck (with the best views) get packed out quickly. Avoid boats that only go as far as Régua – this way you'll only see a bit of the best scenery. There's also a magnificent railway line, the Linha do Douro, which departs from São Bento station and trundles as far as the tiny village of Pocinho in the Alto Douro (3.5 hours). For the first hour it's nondescript suburbia and countryside, but after Régua the railway traces a spectacular course beside the river with glorious views of the vine-combed hillsides. There is not much to see in Pocinho itself, and a more popular option is a train to Pinhão followed by a boat trip along a scenic stretch of the Douro. Bustling Régua, where cruises stop off, also offers river excursions and is home to the Douro Museum, a temple to wine. Whichever way you go, a day-trip by rail demands an early start, and you will need to be highly organized with timing.

Hiring a car has the obvious advantage of flexibility, and this way you are able to enjoy the best of the scenery. However, driving is not for the faint-hearted. Roads are steep, winding and slow-going, so drivers won't be able to take in the vistas, nor taste or imbibe with abandon.

Drinking in the view

# THINGS TO DO

## ENTERTAINMENT

Porto has seen a huge surge in entertainment and especially nightlife options in recent years. The city stages some great music, both classical and contemporary, and downtown Porto is a hive of lively cafés, bars and late-night clubs. In summer look out for flyers advertising concerts in various venues around the city, some of which are free.

### CONCERTS, THEATRE, OPERA AND CINEMA

The iconic **Casa da Música** (Av. da Boavista 604-610; www.casa-damusica.com) is the city's premier venue for local and international classical and contemporary music, and is home to the leading Orquestra Nacional do Porto. The avant-garde concert hall has been a huge success since opening in 2005, and has helped regenerate the Boavista area. Prices for concerts are very reasonable and some are free. In summer, the **Jardim do Palácio de Cristal** and **Serralves Park** stage open-air concerts. The 3000-seat **Coliseu do Porto** (Rua de Passos Manuel 137; www.coliseu.pt) stages international events, from rock and indie concerts to musicals and dance productions.

If you're more into the dance scene, then head beneath the complex to discover old movie theatre turned subterranean club Passos Manuel (Rua de Passos Manuel 137). **Hard Club** in Praça Infante Dom Henrique (www.hardclubporto.com), set within the restored nineteenth-century Ferreira Borges Market, is a dynamic centre with a wide-ranging programme of concerts, dance and theatre events, films, art exhibitions and educational activities. Quite a few events are free of charge.

Local theatre is nearly always in Portuguese. The **Teatro Nacional São João** (see page 41) is the city's main venue, hosting concerts, ballet and occasionally opera, as well as plays.

Multiplexes around the city show mainstream films in English or with English subtitles.

## NIGHTLIFE

Night spots have been springing up all over the city in recent years, with one seemingly on every street corner. Formerly derelict townhouses or abandoned warehouses are now brimming with life, converted – often in vintage style – into cafés, bars or nightclubs (or a combination of all three). Very few clubs show any signs of life before 10pm or 11pm, closing around 4 or even 6am. Admission fees range from €5 to €20 and usually include a drink, though special events will cost extra. Remember to take cash as many places don't accept card.

An irresistible spot for a sundowner is the Ribeira waterfront, watching the twinkling lights across the river from one of the many cafés. In downtown Porto, locals tend to drift from bar to bar, with drink in hand (many venues have plastic cups). Students tend to start their bar crawls at the famous **Café Piolho** (see page 112) by the university. For a late night out, the place to go is 'the Galerias', namely the Rua Galeria de Paris and Rua Cândido dos Reis quarter, which is packed with nightclubs, jazz venues and watering holes of every description. For cocktails created by top mixologists and a cool vibe, try the **Royal Cocktail Club** at Rua da Fábrica 105.

Across the river at Vila Nova de Gaia, **Dick's Bar** at the iconic *Yeatman Hotel* has one of the best cellars in Portugal. The fine wood-aged and vintage ports are available by the bottle or glass. With the plush sofas, jaw-dropping views of Porto and live music Thursday to Saturday, it's hard to drag yourself away. Another Gaia option is the *Terrace Lounge 360°* with panoramic river views at the top of the contemporary **Espaço Porto Cruz** (Largo Miguel Bombarda 23; www.myportocruz.com). Arrive at sunset and watch the sun sinking into the Douro over a cocktail or glass of port.

## Fado

Portugal's musical expression of longing and sorrow is from Lisbon and Coimbra rather than Porto. But there is plenty of *fado vadio*, or amateur *fado*, sung at *fado* houses, tavern-like restaurants offering an evening of song, food and wine. The plaintive Portuguese song, literally 'fate' translated into music, is based on a story or poem and is accompanied by the Portuguese twelve-stringed guitar or *viola* (acoustic Spanish guitar). Lamentation of lost loves, crossed lovers or the forces of destiny are all characteristic themes. Sung by professionals, these chants are plangent, haunting and intensely moving, though to the unattuned ear they can sound strange and monotonous (hence the occasional jollification of traditional *fado* for the benefit of tourists).

*Cálem Port Wine Lodge*

The **Cálem Port Wine Lodge** on the waterfront at Vila Nova de Gaia is one of the main *fado* venues in Porto, staging concerts from Tuesday to Sunday evenings with a cellar tour and tasting included in the price (€21; book online at www.fadoin-porto.com). Alternatively, watch a *fado* show over dinner at the **Taberna Real do Fado** (Rua Dr Barbosa de Castro 58; www.real-fado.pt) or **Casa da Mariquinhas** (Rua de São Sebastião 25; www.

Opulent Café Majestic

casadamariquinhas.pt).
There is usually a minimum
charge for patrons.

## SHOPPING

Porto is becoming increasingly cosmopolitan, with a
clutch of modern shopping
centres and high-street
chains clustered along the
streets. Alongside inter-
national names are the
more interesting young
Portuguese designers showing off their latest creations
as well as eye-catching vintage-style shops. In the streets of Baixa
you can still find the occasional old-fashioned haberdashery, little
altered in 100 years, and thriving old-school grocery shops stacked
with cheeses, spicy sausages and bottles of wine and port.

The favourite street for fashion is the **Rua de Santa Catarina**,
lined with national and international chains, designer boutiques,
jewellery stores, shoe shops and vintage emporiums. When it's
time to take a break, head either for the opulent **Café Majestic**
(see page 111) at No. 112, where the tourist queue normally spills
out on to the road, or *Nata Lisboa* at No. 499, known for its creamy
*pasteis de nata* (custard tarts).

The rejuvenated and pedestrianized **Rua das Flores** is now an
appealing shopping street, with chic cafés, chocolate shops, boutiques, jewellers and antiquarian booksellers. Few can resist the
exquisite delights of the **Chocolataria Ecuador**, a cacao treasure
trove of beautifully packaged Portuguese chocolate bars, truffles,

pralines, macaroons and bonbons. Another favourite is the flagship store of Portuguese cosmetics and fragrance brand **Claus Porto**, an aromatic haven of hand-crafted soaps, candles and cologne (check out the first-floor mini-museum to trace the fascinating journey of the beauty emporium over the decades). Away from the centre, Boavista is known for high-end and designer stores, but lacks the atmosphere of the more central, older streets, with their enchanting Portuguese shops.

## HANDICRAFTS

*Azulejos*, the hand-painted ceramic tiles that have been decorating Portugal's walls through the centuries, make popular souvenirs. Some places will paint tiles to order if you have a particular design in mind, or copy a photograph. Antique *azulejos* are highly sought after and very expensive, but you can buy reproductions of well-known historic designs. Portuguese pottery and ceramics are found in many designs and colours, from fine porcelain to folksy earthenware and the vividly coloured Barcelos rooster.

### Pastéis de nata

You can't go to Portugal and not sample the custard tarts (*pastéis de nata*, in Porto often simply called *nata*). The best ones have a crispy case, a creamy sweet filling and are served straight from the oven. The secret is butter (never margarine), eggs, plenty of sugar, no preservatives – and preferably weeks of training to knead and fold the pastry. One of the best places to try these sweet treats is at *Manteigaria* (Rua de Alexandre Braga 24), where aproned chefs can be seen through the windows rolling out the pastry and stirring huge vats of custard. Listen out for the handbell that signals a fresh-from-the-oven batch of *natas* are on the way.

*Armazém concept store*

For genuine Portuguese products, head to **A Vida Portuguesa** (Rua Galeria de Paris 20; www.avidaportuguesa.com) for everything from retro-wrapped soaps and traditional ceramics to attractively canned sardines. **Armazém** (Rua de Miragaia 93) in a converted riverside port warehouse, is a cool concept store mixing fashion with artwork, antiques and Portuguese-designed crafts and ceramics.

## CORK AND LEATHER

Portugal produces over half the world's cork. While more and more wine bottlers are using screw caps, new uses have been found for eco-friendly Portuguese cork. You can find finely crafted bags, baseball caps, lampshades, hats, handbags and even umbrellas made from cork. The Portuguese leather industry is world-renowned, and belts, bags, purses, wallets, luggage and shoes are good buys. Try the **Feeting Room**, a creative concept store at Largo dos Lóios 86, where Portuguese shoes and boots are beautifully displayed alongside (non-leather) clothing and accessories.

## ART GALLERIES

Northwest of the centre, Rua de Miguel Bombarda and the surrounding area is the place to come for hip galleries, concept stores, vintage clothing, organic food shops and trendy accessories. **Ó! Galeria** at No. 61 is one of the largest galleries, with regularly changing exhibitions of drawings, illustrations, books and magazines, mostly by young and up-and-coming illustrators. At No. 285, the **CCB** (Centro Comercial Bombarda; Mon–Sat noon–8pm) is a hub of independent Portuguese boutiques and galleries. Note that most shops in the quarter don't open until noon.

## BOOKS

The **Livraria Lello** (Rua das Carmelitas 144; www.livrarialello.pt; tickets available online or from the corner shop up the road, redeemable against purchases) near the Clérigos Tower is a must-see for any visitor to Porto (see page 46). The Art Nouveau bookstore dates back to 1906 and is rated one of the most beautiful in the world, so be prepared for crowds. The fabulous collection includes limited-edition books. A 10-minute walk towards the river takes you to the family-owned **Livraria Chaminé de Mota** (Rua das Flores 28; www.bit.ly/livariachaminé), a literary wonderland of second-hand and antiquarian books concealed behind an unassuming lemon-yellow facade. Ask to see the incredible collection of typewriters, maps, music boxes, gramophones and old printing paraphernalia on the upper floors.

## GASTRONOMY

The atmospheric **Mercado do Bolhão**, dating from 1914, has always been the place to go for the freshest of fish, meat, fruit and veg, as well as chickens, tripe and rabbits. But the wrought-iron market hall, in dire need of restoration, shuttered in 2018 and was still closed at the time of writing in 2022. With modern shops and restaurants planned for the upper tier, it is unlikely to reopen as the earthy market of yore. The market stalls have been moved to the **Bolhão Temporary Market** (Rua de Fernandes Tomás; Mon–Fri 8am–8pm, Sat until 6pm), just 200m from the original.

The surrounding streets also have some enticing traditional grocery stores, such as the 100-year-old **A Pérola do Bolhão**, with

*A Pérola do Bolhão*

its handsome Art Nouveau facade on Rua Formosa, opposite the old market. This and other delis will vacuum-pack produce to make it easier for you to take home. **Comer e Chorar Por Mais** ('Eat and Cry for More') at Rua Formosa 300 is another gourmet grocery, jam-packed with hams, cheeses, olive oil, honey, fine wines and freshly made bread from the wood oven.

The Portuguese have a very sweet tooth, and the Portuenses are no exception. The city has myriad patisseries which lure you in with their displays of cakes and pastries. Beware though – they can be very sickly. One of the best confectioners is **Arcádia** on Rua do Almada 63 (west of Aliados), family-run since 1933 and famous for chocolate *linguas de gato* (cat's tongues) and rich chocolate and port bonbons, made in partnership with port-producers, Calém.

Port is the obvious souvenir to take back home if luggage permits. If not, it can be shipped for you – at a price. Vintage port from the most select years is what connoisseurs and collectors seek, but there are much cheaper bottles available. Look for aged tawny, LBV (late bottle vintages) or a bottle of white port. The dry version of the latter is now popularly drunk in Porto with tonic water and a slice of orange or lemon, especially in the summer months. Dozens of outlets sell port and you can try it at wine lodges, tasting rooms and some of the shops. **Portologia**, at Rua de São João 28–30, just up from the Ribeira waterfront, is a small and cosy port-tasting place with knowledgeable staff to guide you through the vast range. They have over 200 ports, mainly from the smaller producers, and offer a set price for tastings so you can taste before purchasing (think six tastings for €25 or €35, depending on the quality of the port).

For tasting and/or buying regional wines as well as port, head for the **Instituto dos Vinhos do Douro e do Porto** (Douro Wine and Port Institute; Rua Ferreira Borges 27; www.ivdp.pt). With a wine shop, small museum and tastings, this is an excellent introduction to port and Douro wines.

# CHILDREN'S PORTO

With its vintage trams, funiculars and river trips, Porto offers some great ways to entertain kids around the city. Take them on Tram #1, which rattles alongside the river to the beaches at Foz do Douro, or on a boat trip to see the six bridges of Porto (see page 73). The top children's attractions in the centre are the **World of Discoveries** (see page 54) and **Sea Life** (1a Rua Particular do Castelo do Queijo; www.sealife-porto.pt; Mon–Fri 10am–6pm, Sat–Sun 10am–6.15pm, last entry 45 mins before closing), a large aquarium where you can come nose to nose with sharks, rays and sea turtles.

Porto has plenty of green spaces where young ones can let off steam. The **Jardim do Palácio de Cristal** has a lake, artificial caves and strutting peacocks. Further west, the vast **Parque da Cidade** (City Park) stretches as far as the coast and is a favourite spot for locals to stroll, jog, cycle or picnic. The park has ponds populated with ducks, swans and geese, as well as a Water Pavilion which featured in Lisbon's Expo '98. Children can have fun with the interactive games, aimed to educate in the importance of water. Exhibits show how a tornado is formed and teach young inquisitive minds about the water cycle.

In Vila Nova de Gaia, the **Santo Inácio Zoo** (www.zoosantoinacio.com) has a free shuttle bus service four times a day between April and October, departing near Porto's Sé and taking around 15 minutes. The zoo is home to around 300 species and includes a lion enclosure with a glass tunnel where the magnificent creatures walk above you. The animals are not too restricted and there are lakes, pleasant green areas and prairie dogs roaming free.

# SPORTS AND OUTDOOR PURSUITS

## FOOTBALL

FC Porto (or simply Porto) is one of 'the Big Three' in Portugal, alongside Lisbon's Benfica and Sporting CP. In international matches, Porto is the most decorated team in Portugal. They won the UEFA European Champions League (or European Cup) in 1987 and 2004, the UEFA Super Cup in 1987, the UEFA Cup/European League in 2003 and 2011 and the Intercontinental Cup in 1987 and 2004. Local supporters are called Portistas.

Home matches are played at the **Estádio do Dragão** (metro Estádio do Dragão; www.fcporto.pt), which was built 4km northeast of the city centre for the 2004 European Championships. Stadium tours with audio guides in seven languages are available on non-match days (on the hour Tues–Sun 11am–5pm, Mon 3–5pm) and include entrance to a museum on the club's history.

## SWIMMING AND SURFING

The chilly waters and choppy waves of the Atlantic tend to put off casual swimmers, but there are opportunities for surfers and plentiful places to just chill out. The best beach near Porto is Espinho,

20km to the south of the city and accessed in about half an hour by rail from Porto. It's an 8km stretch, particularly popular with surfers. Closer to Porto, Foz do Douro has easily reachable beaches with sand, but most also have rocky outcrops. Sunloungers are normally available to hire, and there are plenty of beaches with bars and snacks.

Matosinhos has a large sandy swathe which attracts learner surfers but, being close to a big port, it's not everyone's first choice. Further north are better sandy beaches at Vila do Conde and Póvoa de Varzim. The popular surfing spots have surf schools which hire out gear and provide group or private lessons. The most appealing swimming pools in the area are the sea pools at Leça da Palmeira (see page 80), carved into the rocks and sprayed with Atlantic foam on windy days.

*FC Porto and Sporting CP playing in the 2021/22 Taça de Portugal semifinal*

## BIRDWATCHING

The **Reserva Natural Local do Estuário do Douro** (dawn–dusk, www.parquebiologico.pt; free) is a small nature reserve on the Douro estuary in Vila Nova de Gaia. It is home to over 200 species of bird, among them kingfishers, herons, white egrets, sandpipers, plovers, red knots and blue throats.

## GOLF

The oldest golf club in the Iberian peninsula, founded by the British in the late nineteenth century, is the Oporto Golf Club in Espinho, Vila Nova de Gaia, which is located 18km from the centre of Porto. Also in Vila Nova de Gaia is the 9-hole Miramar Golf Club (Av. Sacadura Cabral, Arcozelo), situated 12km from the city centre.

### THE LONGEST NIGHT OF THE YEAR

If – out of the blue – someone hits you on the head with a leek or a squeaky plastic hammer, you'll know it's the Festa de São João. This festival, with strong pagan traditions (despite celebrating St John the Baptist, patron saint of the city), takes place annually on the night of 23rd/24th June. Thousands of partygoers descend on the centre of Porto to make merry. Streets are strung with bunting, colourful lights sparkle in the squares, wine flows and sardines are barbecued on every street corner. Street parties, free concerts and dancing are all part of the scene. At midnight, a dazzling firework display erupts over the River Douro. The revellers who are still going drift along the riverside to Foz to watch the sunrise in the early morning. Fortunately for all, 24th June is a public holiday in Porto and the climax of the festa is the colourful regatta of the *barcos rabelos* on the River Douro.

# WHAT'S ON

**Fantasporto (or 'Fantas')** February/March. A 10-day international film festival screening fantasy, sci-fi and horror movies.

**Queima das Fitas do Porto (Porto's Burning of the Ribbons)** May. Final-year student festival featuring concerts, academic parades and other events which now involve the entire city.

**Festa de São João** June 23rd/24th. Porto's biggest event of the year (see page 96) and part of the Festas da Cidade, which has events and entertainment throughout the month.

**Regata dos Rabelos** June 24th (coinciding with the Festa de São João). A regatta of the barcos rabelos (wooden sail boats) which once ferried port wine down the River Douro.

**Serralves em Festa** Early June. Forty hours of non-stop dance, music, theatre and exhibitions in Serralves Park; also in Baixa. This is the largest contemporary arts festival in Portugal with both International and Portuguese performers (www.serralvesemfesta.com).

**Nos Primavera Sound** June. Two-day open-air music festival in Parque da Cidade (www.nosprimaverasound.com).

**Feira do Livro do Porto (Porto Book Fair)** June. A long-established event, traditionally held at the Jardim do Palácio de Cristal.

**São Pedro da Afurada** 29 June. Festival in honour of St Peter, patron saint of fishermen, at the fishing village of Afurada, Vila Nova de Gaia.

**Festival Internacional de Folclore Cidade** Late July/early August. Week-long folklore festival.

**LGBT Porto Pride** First or second week of July. LGBTQ+ celebration first held in Porto in 2001, with a parade since 2006.

**Porto Wine Fest** July. Wine tastings and gastronomic events on the riverbank of Vila Nova de Gaia.

**Noites Ritual Rock** Last weekend of August. Rock concerts by local bands held in the Jardim do Palácio de Cristal.

**Porta Jazz** Early December. Free jazz concerts (www.portajazz.com).

**Christmas** December. Fairs and markets around the city.

# FOOD AND DRINK

Culinary hotspots have been springing up all over the city in recent years, and there is now a great diversity in the dining scene. You can choose from trusty hole-in-the-wall *tascas* (taverns), tapas bars and new on-trend restaurants where creative chefs have developed a more refined, cosmopolitan style of cuisine. The region is rich in culinary delights, with fish from the Atlantic, pork and dairy produce from the remote Trás-os-Montes ('Beyond the Mountains') and the famous port and wines from the valley of the Upper Douro. But Porto's own specialities are still very much on the menu. You won't have to go far to find *tripas à moda do Porto* (Port-style tripe) or the *francesinha*, a multi-layered gut-busting sandwich (see page 105).

## WHERE TO EAT

Formal restaurants are few and far between, the emphasis being more on smaller places serving *petiscos* (smaller versions of large dishes, like tapas but usually larger). Two or three of these can provide a decent meal, there are plenty to choose from and it's the perfect way of trying a handful of regional dishes. Typical *petiscos* include *pataniscas* (salt-cod croquettes), *gambas al ajillo* (garlic shrimps) or *salada de polvo* (octopus salad).

Tascas are typically found in the narrow streets of the old town, and are traditionally family-run joints with paper tablecloths, serving hearty helpings of authentic Portuguese cuisine. Often one portion suffices for two. Some *tascas* have seen a modern makeover in recent years, but they remain faithful to local fare, albeit with a modern twist. The inconspicuous backstreet eateries are usually better value than the touristy restaurants and the cafés strung along the quaysides, on both sides of the river.

A *restaurante* covers a whole range of eateries, from sumptu-ous to basic. A *churrasqueira* is a grill, typically serving simple eats such as grilled sardines or half chickens. A *marisqueira* will special-ize in seafood; a *cervejaria* is a beer house, which normally serves seafood and steaks as well as a good choice of beers; and a *confei-taria* is a patisserie. Prices across the range of restaurants are fairly affordable by the standards of European capitals.

Porto has a vibrant café culture, with countless places offering the simple pleasure of a cup of good coffee and creamy *pastéis de nata* (custard tarts) or other freshly made pastries.

### Pre-starters and starters

No sooner are you seated than unrequested pre-starters such as bread, fresh cheese, cured ham, olives and maybe fish paté or

*The francesinha, a gut-busting sandwich and Porto speciality*

octopus salad will arrive on the table. They may seem free, but they are not. It may only be a euro or two for bread (often delicious Broa or corn bread) or olives, but it could be €5 for the cheese or meat. These often make appetizing starters, but you have the option (if you're strong-willed!) to leave them untouched and not be charged.

Local starters include seafood dishes, hearty soups, cured and smoked hams, sausages and salamis, often heavily smoked and spiced. The ubiquitous *caldo verde* soup, made with finely shredded cabbage, potatoes, onion, garlic and sometimes sausage, features on menus from the classiest restaurants down to the humblest *tasca*. Thick bread soups are a meal in themselves and include the classic *açorda de marisco*, a spicy, garlicky shellfish stew.

Bacalhau à gomes de sá

### Fish and seafood

Seafood enthusiasts will be spoilt for choice. You'll find sardines and squid, clams and crabs, sea bass, lobster and sole. The humble but noble Portuguese sardine is an inexpensive standard, and served with a hulk of local rustic bread and a bottle of house wine, you can still feast well on a small budget. The sardine season, when the fish are at their fattest, is from May to October. Seafood restaurants generally sell shellfish by weight, giving the price in euros

per kilo. Among the specialities are *caldeirada de peixe*, a
rich seafood stew, and *arroz
de marisco*, a delicious seafood rice crammed with
crab, lobster claws, prawns,
clams and cockles. Clams
are often served simply with
crushed garlic cloves, fresh
coriander and white wine:
*amêijoas à Bulhão Pato*. Squid
(*lulas*) often comes stuffed
with rice, olives, tomato and
onion, though the large squid
are often grilled and served

> ## Portuguese portions
>
> The locals have large
> appetites. Expect huge
> helpings, especially of
> casserole dishes of say cod,
> *cataplanas* or tripe, where
> one portion could easily feed
> two or even three. Some
> restaurants will offer a half
> portion, *uma meia dose*, and
> unless you are absolutely
> starving the smaller portion
> is usually sufficient.

on a skewer with prawns (*gambas*). You can't normally tell from
the menu whether the fish is fresh or frozen, but you can always
ask the waiter for the catch of the day. Don't assume the bass and
bream are from the high seas – much of it is farmed these days.
Serious fish aficionados should head for Matosinhos, famous for
its fresh fish restaurants (see page 75).

The national favourite fish is curiously neither Portuguese nor
eaten fresh: it's dried, salted cod or *bacalhau* and is served in
100, 365 or 1000 different ways, depending on the teller's taste
for hyperbole. Records show that the Portuguese were fishing
Newfoundland's Grand Banks for cod within just a few years of
Columbus's discovery of America. They were soon to discover that
by salting cod at sea they could make it last the long voyage home.
It was then sun-dried into board-stiff slabs that could be kept for
months. The Portuguese now import *bacalhau* from Norway, just
to be able to meet their annual demands. This, of course, puts the
price of salt cod – once an inexpensive staple of the national diet

*Home-made sausages*

– beyond the reach of the very people it sustained for centuries. All these once-humble recipes are served today in the most expensive restaurants. The Porto speciality is *bacalhau à gomes de sá*: flaky chunks of cod baked with parsley, potatoes, onions and olives and garnished with grated hard-boiled egg.

## Meat dishes

Although the emphasis is on fish and seafood, restaurants do not skimp on meat. The ubiquitous *tripas à moda do Porto* is a thick, hearty stew with offal, white beans and sausages, though every Porto family has its own recipe. The people of Porto are known as *tripeiros* or tripe-eaters (see page 18), but some of the new chefs are catering more for tourists and dropping tripe from the menu. Pork is sweet and tender; ham (*presunto* and *fiambre*) and sausages (*salsichas*) are highly prized in Portugal; and charcuterie features prominently in soups and stews. *Alheira* is a sausage made of meats other than pork (usually chicken) with bread and spices. It was created by the Jewish community in northeast Portugal during the Inquisition to give the impression they had converted to Christianity by eating pork – the traditional ingredient for a Portuguese sausage.

*Arouquesa* veal is succulent and chicken (*frango*) is popular and versatile, whether stewed in wine sauce, fried, roasted or barbecued. *Feijoada* is not nearly as elaborate or ritualized as it is in Portugal's former colony of Brazil, where it is a national dish, but it's still a tasty stew of pigs' trotters, sausage, white beans and cabbage.

## Desserts and cheese

The Portuguese have a passion for all things sweet, and Porto is packed with *pastelerias* (patisseries), bakeries and cafés selling wickedly calorific cakes and pastries. Many of these are loaded with sugar and egg yolks. It was nuns of Portugal in the seventeenth and eighteenth centuries who became famous for creating egg desserts, which explains names such as 'bacon from heaven' (*toucinho do céu*), nuns' tummies (*barriga da freira*) and angels' cheeks (*papos d'anjo*). As in the rest of Portugal, the crispy and creamy custard tarts, called *pastéis de nata* (in Porto simply *nata*) feature in every patisserie and on nearly

*Porto is synonymous with port wine*

*Super Bock beer*

every menu. Egg desserts and pastries are flavoured with cinnamon, lemon, orange or almonds, and each is shaped in its own traditional way, for example like miniature haystacks, or occasionally even lamprey eels. The Portuguese so love this ugly river fish that they make golden egg effigies of it for festive occasions.

The Portuguese find that nothing complements – or follows – an egg sweet as well as a silky, syrupy wine, usually a vintage port or a Madeira, but better still a good, strong cup of coffee to cut the sweetness.

The most savoury Portuguese cheeses are from ewes' milk. Serra da Estrela is the richest and most expensive cheese and can be served fresh or cured.

## Wine

Portuguese wine has come on in leaps and bounds in recent years. The Douro Valley, traditionally best known for port, now produces some wonderfully robust and full-bodied reds, as well as some excellent whites. From the Minho region comes *vinho verde,* a refreshing, slightly sparkling young wine which goes down a treat with seafood on a sun-drenched day. *Vinho espumante* is Portuguese sparkling wine, packaged in a champagne-shaped bottle. Most are sweetish, but you can find some quite dry versions too. When ordering wine you can't go far wrong with the house wine (*vinho da casa*). Ask the waiter for *tinto* (red), *branco* (white) or *rosado* (pink).

## Port

Fortified port wine has tantalized palates around the world since the British began exporting it in the seventeenth century. It comes in many forms, from ruby, tawny, white, rosé and late bottled vintage (LBV) through to vintage port, generally considered to be

---

### PORTO'S SANDWICH SPECIAL

The *francesinha* or 'little Frenchie' is a glorified sandwich consisting of chunks of steak, cured ham and sausage between slices of white bread, swathed in melted cheese, drenched in a thick spicy tomato and beer sauce, topped with a fried egg and (optionally) accompanied by French fries. It sounds more American than Portuguese, but in fact was invented in the 1950s by an emigrant returning from France where he had worked as a chef. Back in Portugal, he decided to try an elaborate version of the *croque monsieur* for the Portuguese. Locals all have their favourite *francesinha* restaurant, usually based on the quality of the meat and the sauce (a secret recipe that varies from place to place). You can find the dish in dozens of cafés and restaurants – just make sure you don't have to eat another meal on the same day.

### Fixed menus

To fill up for a few euros, opt for the *menu do dia* (fixed menu) offered by many restaurants at lunch time, often at a fraction of the cost of the evening meal. A set menu typically offers soup and bread, a main course and a glass of wine. Also well worth trying is the *prato do dia* or dish of the day.

the finest of them all. Before dinner, try a P&T, *porto tónico* (white port and tonic), which is currently all the rage as a summer cocktail. The wine tasting lodges are all in Vila Nova de Gaia, across the Douro from Porto, offering wine tours and tastings (see page 66), but there are countless places in Porto to taste port, often with a sommelier on hand to explain the nuances of smooth tawny ports, fruity rubies and sweet or dry whites. The Port and Douro Wines Institute (see page 33) is a good place to sample them.

## Other drinks

Super Bock beer, brewed in Porto, is good and refreshing, very like Lisbon's Sagres. If you want a draft beer and want to sound like a local, ask for a *fino*. As in many other parts of Europe, Portugal has followed the fashion for craft beers and there are plenty of different types to try.

## Coffee

Coffeehouses are a Portuguese national institution, a gathering place morning, noon and night. This is not surprising in a country whose former colonies – Brazil and Angola – still produce some of the finest coffee beans in the world. The choice may be a *cimbalino,* a powerful espresso, or a *carioca,* a weaker version, which with a drop of milk is a *garoto*. If you want plenty of milk, ask for a *galão*, which comes small (*pequeno*) or tall (*grande*).

## TO HELP YOU ORDER...

Could we have a table? **Queremos uma mesa?**
Do you have a set-price menu? **Tem uma ementa turística?**
I'd like a/an/some… **Queria**…

beer **uma cerveja**
the bill a **conta**
bread **pão**
butter **manteiga**
dessert **sobremesa**
fish **peixe**
fruit **fruta**
ice-cream **gelado**
meat **carne**
the menu **a carta**
milk **leite**
mineral water **água mineral**

napkin **guardanapo**
pepper **pimenta**
potatoes **batatas**
salad **salada**
salt **sal**
sandwich **sanduíche**
soup **sopa**
sugar **açúcar**
tea **chá**
vegetables **legumes**
wine **vinho**
wine list **carta de vinos**

## MENU READER

**alho** garlic
**amêijoas** baby clams
**arroz** rice
**assado** roast, baked
**bacalhau** cod
**besugo** sea bream
**dobrada** tripe
**dourada** sea bass
**feijões** beans
**frito** fried
**gambas** prawns
**lagosta** spiny lobster
**lenguado** sole
**lombo** fillet

**lulas** squid
**mariscos** shellfish
**mexilhões** mussels
**ostras** oysters
**ovo** egg
**pescada** hake
**pescadinha** whiting
**polvos** baby octopus
**queijo** cheese
**salmonete** red mullet
**truta** trout
**vitela** veal

# WHERE TO EAT

The prices indicated here are for a two-course meal with wine for one person. Note that some fish or shellfish dishes will be more expensive. Tax (IVA) is included. Restaurants listed here accept major credit cards unless cash only is stated.

| | |
|---|---|
| €€€€ | **over 45 euros** |
| €€€ | **30–45 euros** |
| €€ | **20–30 euros** |
| € | **below 20 euros** |

## RIBEIRA

**Adega de São Nicolau €€** *Rua de São Nicolau;* www.facebook.com/AdegaS-Nicolau. Tucked away down a narrow alley just back from the riverfront, this cosy restaurant is designed as an upturned hull of a ship. A favourite with locals, the kitchen serves up authentic Porto dishes, including salted codfish croquettes, Porto-style tripe (one helping is easily big enough for two), octopus rice and *aronquera* veal steak. Mon–Sat noon–11pm.

**Bacalhau €€** *Muro dos Bacalhoeiros 153-155; tel: 222 010 521.* No surprises as to the speciality here. You can start with *sopa alentejana com lascas de bacalhau* – Alentejo soup with cods' tongues – then pick from at least three *bacalhau* main dishes. If you're not a fan, meat dishes are also available. Servings are all huge so ask for a half-portion or share. The trio of tables at this hole-in-the-wall, right over the river, are highly sought-after in summer. Sun–Thurs 11am–11pm, Fri & Sat till midnight.

**ODE Porto Wine House €€€€** *Largo do Terreiro 7*; www.odeporto.com. Fine dining in a romantic little restaurant with medieval stone walls, beams and candlelit tables. The emphasis is on slow food based on dishes cooked by the owner's grandmother and mother, and given a modern twist. Ingredients are sourced from local farmers using traditional methods, and all the dishes are cooked in a small open-view kitchen. Cash only. Tues–Sun 7–11pm, Fri & Sat till midnight.

**Traça €€** *Largo de São Domingos 88*; www.restaurantetraca.com. Stylish restaurant in a seventeenth-century building serving authentic Iberian fare such as *salpicão de caça* (smoked sausage made from game), *maozinhas de porco* (pigs' trotters), *cabrito* (kid) and *polvo em vinho do Porto e grelos* (octopus with port wine sauce and turnip tops). Slow food is the name of the game. For more conventional tastes there are crispy prawns, steaks and pork. Weekday lunchtime set menus are good value. Mon–Fri noon–11pm, Sat & Sun 12.30–11pm.

# BAIXA

**Caldeireiros €** *Rua dos Caldeireiros 139*; www.facebook.com/Caldeireiros. Bustling restaurant with communal tables and a good choice of *petiscos* (tapas). Try the *alheira de caça* (game sausage), *petingas* (tiny fish), grilled octopus salad, tripe Porto-style, salt-cod croquettes or steak. Mon–Sat 12.30–3.30pm & 6pm–1am.

**Cantina 32 €€–€€€** *Rua das Flores 32*; www.cantina32.com. Trendy restaurant on the attractive Rua das Flores, with industrial-chic setting, long shared tables and Portuguese specialities. Plenty of options for vegetarians. Mon–Sat 12.30–3pm & 6.30–11pm.

**Cantinho do Avillez €€€** *Rua Mouzinho da Silveira 166*; www.cantinhodoavillez.pt. Star chef José Avillez opened this restaurant in the centre of Porto following the success of his restaurants in Lisbon. Decor is cheerful and casual, the cuisine simple but sophisticated. Among his celebrated dishes are the giant Algarve red shrimps with Thai flavours; flaked cod with bread crumbs, LT egg and 'exploding' olives; and the Barrosã PDO hamburger. For a decadent dessert try the Hazelnut Trio. Mon–Fri 12.30–3pm & 7pm–midnight, Sat & Sun 12.30pm–midnight.

**Dama Pé de Cabra €** *Passeio de São Lázaro 5*; www.facebook.com/damapedecabra. Small, charming café 10 minutes' walk east of São Bento station, which makes a great spot for breakfast or brunch. Try the delicious flavoured breads (chestnut, pumpkin seed and carrot), home-made jams, scrambled eggs, superior sandwiches or lovely platters of cheese and cured meats. Tues–Sat 9.30am–3.30pm, Fri & Sat also 7.30–10pm.

**DOP €€€€** *Palácio das Artes, Largo São Domingos 18*; www.ruipaula.com. Leading chef Rui Paula describes the dishes at his elegant restaurant within a palace as 'cheerful, colourful and fragrant'. Try octopus carpaccio with pomegranate or sea-bass ceviche followed perhaps by lobster and fish risotto or veal cheek with gnocchi. Two tasting menus, 'Memory' and 'Sea', both with wine pairing, are weekday lunch options. Mon 12.30–3pm, Tues–Sat 12.30–3pm &7.30–11pm.

**Ernesto €€** *Rua da Picaria 85; tel: 222 002 600*. Established in 1938, this family restaurant is a favourite with locals for its authentic Portuguese fare such as *bacalhau*, grilled octopus, tripe Porto-style, roast kid and veal. Friendly service and attractive setting with wooden beams, stone walls and modern art. Mon 8.30am–3.30pm, Tues–Sat 8.30am–3.30pm & 6.30pm–midnight.

**Escondidinho Do Barredo €** *Rua Canastreiros 28; tel: 222 057 229. Escondidinho* means hidden – and hidden it really is. Don't look for the name, look for the red door. The simple homely *taberna* is run by two delightful sisters (who don't speak English) and has an open kitchen serving *petiscos* (tapas) for the more adventurous tastes: tripe, pigs' ears, octopus, as well as *bolinhos de bacalhau* (codfish cakes) and sardines, all of which can be washed down with amazingly cheap house wine. Very popular with locals and always busy. Tues–Sun 9am–11pm.

**Gruta €€€** *Rua de Santa Catarina 112;* www.grutaporto.com. With bare stone walls and pale wood accents, *Gruta* is a stylish hangout for a glass of wine and a bite to eat. The focus is on the bounty of the sea, with plenty of fresh, sustainably sourced fish and seafood on the menu; think octopus carpaccio or langoustine bisque followed by *moqueca* (Brazilian fish stew) or seafood rice with squid, shrimp and clams. A handful of veggie dishes spans the likes of beetroot risotto and home-made ravioli. Friendly staff offer excellent recommendations for wine pairings; female-owned and -run. Tues–Sat 7.30am–10pm, Sat also 12.30–2.30pm.

**Café Guarany €€€** *Avenida dos Aliados 85-89*; www.cafeguarany.com. From the team that gave us the famous *Café Majestic* (see opposite), *Café Guarany* serves the same pastries as its sibling – but at much cheaper prices. Not just for sweet treats, the restaurant also serves fish and meat dishes. On the main

Avenida dos Aliados, this is a historical brasserie-style café, established in 1933 and traditionally a haunt of musicians. Expect live music and entertainment on Friday and Saturday nights. Daily 9am–midnight.

**Lado B Café €** *Rua Passos Manuel 190/192*; www.ladobcafe.pt. On Rua Passos Manuel, *Santiago* (see page 112) may be the most famous haunt for *francesinha*, but *Lado B*, another no-frills diner, is pretty good too and rarely as crowded. You'll need to try both to see if you agree with its claim: '*A melhor francesinha do mundo*' ('The best francesinha in the world'). Other options are burgers, steak sandwiches and salads. Skip breakfast and come with a large appetite. Mon–Thurs 11am–11.30pm, Fri & Sat till 2am.

**Café Majestic €€** *Rua de Santa Catarina 112*; www.cafemajestic.com. Dating back to 1921 and a former haunt of Porto's literati, this elegant café is today on every tourist's bucket list and there is nearly always a queue outside for a table. It's probably the most expensive café in Porto but the opulent Belle Époque interior and the *rubanadas* (French toast with creamy egg custard) are hard to resist. Mon–Sat 9am–11.30pm.

**Manso €€€** *Rua Professor Mota Pinto 170*; www.instagram.com/mansorestaurant. With local artwork hung on the walls, Portuguese wine bottles lining the shelves and supper clubs starring emerging chefs, *Manso* feels like a community venture building up and supporting other Porto creatives. The team whip up inventive Portuguese dishes with an Asian twist, ferment their own kimichi and will even pick dishes for adventurous diners – you might end up with *bacalhau* with *pil pil*, perhaps, or maybe the *gamba tartare* with a slick of horseradish. Wed–Sun noon–3pm & 7.30–11pm.

**Meia-Nau Porto €€€** *Tv de Cedofeita 48*; www.meianaurestaurante.com. The younger sibling to the Matosinhos original, *Meia-Nau Porto* brought its winning combination of fresh fish and lively buzz to the city centre in 2021. The seafood-dominated menu remains the same, but there's an outdoor terrace and a new chef: Pedro Silva. Opt for the signature grilled fish, which, depending on that day's catch, might be squid, sardines, horse mackerel, salmon, sea bass, turbot, sole or grouper, served with rice and vegetables or potatoes and salad. Much of the seafood has been rustled into traditional Portuguese dishes too. Tues–Sun noon–3pm & 7–10pm.

**Café Piolho €** *Praça de Parada Leitão 45*; www.cafepiolho.com. Even though its official name is *Café Âncora D'Ouro* (and that's the name it has outside), everyone calls it *Café Piolho*. Dating from 1909, it is well known as a meeting place for university students and teachers, and also for demos during the dictatorship. Very popular, particularly on Friday and Saturday evenings when students meet here for the first drink of the night. Mon–Sat 7am–4am.

**Café Santiago €** *Rua Passos Manuel 226*; www.cafesantiago.pt. This basic café is renowned for Porto's speciality: the meat-filled, multi-layered *francesinha*, covered in melted cheese, topped with a fried egg, drenched in a dark sauce and accompanied by chips, if you wish. Be prepared for queues at weekends or go to the less crowded *Lado B* (see page 111). Mon–Sat noon–11pm.

**Semea by Euskalduna €€** *Cais das Pedras 15*; www.semeabyeuskalduna. pt. A lovely riverside location, a local-leaning menu and dreamy interiors combine to excellent effect at *Semea*. Sage-green walls and a wild foliage arrangement suspended from the ceiling create a warm Scandi vibe, with pale wooden tables spilling outside onto a waterside deck. The kitchen showcases fresh fish and seafood, along with reinvented Portuguese classics such as stuffed veal tongue or pork head. Don't miss the signature French toast. Tues 7pm–midnight, Wed–Sat noon–3pm & 7pm–midnight.

## MASSARELOS

**Antiqvvm €€€€** *Rua de Entrequintas 220*; www.antiqvvm.pt. Michelin-starred cuisine, fine wines and river views steal the show at this elegant restaurant beside the Museu Romântico. Chef Vitor Matos reimagines traditional Portuguese cuisine, and each dish is artfully presented. Choose from the fixed-price lunch menu, tasting menus at €90 and €120 (with paired wines) or à la carte. A glassed-in gallery opens on to a large courtyard for alfresco dining in warm weather. Tues–Sat noon–midnight, Sun noon–3pm; terrace open Sun 3–7pm.

**Rota do Chá €** *Rua Miguel Bombarda 457*; www.rotadocha.com. A tea lover's haven in the artsy Bombarda quarter. Choose from over 300 blends (staff are on hand if you're bamboozled) and sip tea in one of the tranquil spaces or the hidden garden, maybe with a slice of chocolate caramel pie or an apple muffin. Don't just pop in for a quick cuppa – everything is slow and mindful here, including the service. Mon–Sat 11am–8pm, Sun noon–8pm.

## VILA NOVA DE GAIA

**Barão Fladgate €€€€** *Rua do Choupelo 250*; www.baraofladgate.com. Named after John Fladgate, a nineteenth-century Port shipper, Taylor's port wine lodge restaurant combines fine wining and dining with glorious views across the Douro River to Porto. Ideally, visit the Port Cellars first (see page 67) then enjoy a languid lunch or dinner at the restaurant. Set week-day lunches are good value. Daily 12.30–3pm & 7.30–10.30pm.

**Vinum Restaurant €€€€** *Graham's Port Lodge, Rua do Agro 141*; www.vinumatgrahams.com. A seductive spot combining dazzling views down to the river, the best dishes of the Douro, Trás-os-Montes, the Minho and the Atlantic and, of course, expert wine pairings with bottles from the famous Graham's cellars. The menu features fish fresh from Matosinhos Market and rare Vaca Velha beef from Trás-os-Montes. *Vinum* also has a wine bar offering lighter meals and sharing plates. Daily 12.30–4pm & 6.30–11pm .

**The Yeatman €€€€** *Rua do Choupelo 88*; www.the-yeatman-hotel.com. Part of the famous *Yeatman* hotel, this is a favourite destination of oenophiles and gourmands. It is the only restaurant in Porto with two Michelin stars, offers perfect food and wine pairings and has gorgeous views over Porto and the River Douro. Chef Ricardo Costa showcases the best of Portuguese products, laying emphasis on local produce and giving traditional dishes an innovative twist. Daily 12.30–3pm & 7.30–11pm.

## BEYOND PORTO
### Leça da Palmeira

**Casa de Chá da Boa Nova €€€€** *Avenida da Liberdade No 1681, Leça da Palmeira*; www.casadechadaboanova.pt. This incredible teahouse (*casa de chà*) is a National Monument. A seductive and sleek structure built into the rocks above the sea, it is designed by Portugal's leading architect Álvaro Siza Vieira. Choose from three tasting menus: Land and Sea, Atlantic or Boa

Nova, with optional wine pairings, and be prepared for a hefty bill. Original and interesting combinations, such as eel and date foie gras or line-caught hake with plankton and barnacles have earned Porto-born chef Rui Paula a Michelin star. Reservations are essential to nab a table. Mon 7.30–11pm, Tues–Sat 12.30–3pm & 7.30–11pm.

## Foz do Douro

**Bocca €€–€€€** *Rua do Passeio Alegre 3; tel: 226 170 004.* This contemporary glass box has a terrace and fabulous waterfront setting overlooking the River Douro. The food is Italian-inspired and the decor sophisticated. Fish dishes include gambas, salmon ceviche, mussels in brandy and *corvina* with coriander rice; also delicious crusty pizzas from the wood-burning oven and an excellent choice of Portuguese wines.

**Pedro Lemos €€€€** *Rua do Padre Luís Cabral 974*; www.pedrolemos.net. Hidden away in the old town of Foz, Pedro Lemos' eponymous Michelin-star restaurant is a foodie haven, with exquisite dishes centring around set menus of five or seven courses, plus desserts. Tues–Sat 12.30–3pm & 7.30–11pm.

**Tavi €** *Rua Senhora da Lux 363, Foz do Douro*; www.tavi.pt. Ocean views (if you can get a terrace seat) and fabulous cakes and pastries lure tourists to *Tavi*. Good for brunch and for sunsets over the Atlantic. Daily 8.30am–8pm.

## Matoshinos

**Esplanada Marisqueira A Antiga €€€€** *Rua Roberto Ivens 628*; www.esplanadamarisqueira.com. If you want to splash out on a gourmet fish restaurant this is the place to go. Excellent catch of the day, and the seafood platter is to die for. Booking advised. Daily noon–1am.

**Salta o Muro €** *Rua Heróis de Franca 386*; tel: 229 380 870. Typical of Matoshinos's fish restaurants, this is an unassuming, bustling family-run place, packed with locals and tourists in the know. Favourite fish dishes are octopus with rice, *caldeirada* (fish soup), sardines and turbot – all simply cooked, fresh and delicious. Not much English is spoken, but there's a list with fish translated into English. Excellent value. Tues–Sat 12.15–3pm & 7–11pm.

# TRAVEL ESSENTIALS

## PRACTICAL INFORMATION

**A** Accessible travel **116**

Accommodation **116**

Airport **117**

**B** Bicycle hire **117**

Budgeting for your trip **118**

**C** Camping **119**

Car hire **119**

Climate **119**

Clothing **120**

Crime and safety **120**

**D** Driving **120**

**E** Electricity **121**

Embassies and consulates **121**

Emergencies **122**

**G** Getting there **122**

Guides and tours **123**

**H** Health and medical care **124**

**L** Language **125**

LGBTQ+ travellers **125**

**M** Maps **126**

Media **126**

Money matters **126**

**O** Opening hours **127**

**P** Police **127**

Post offices **128**

Public holidays **128**

**R** Religion **129**

**T** Telephones **129**

Time zones **129**

Tipping **130**

Toilets **130**

Tourist information **130**

Transport **131**

**V** Visas and entry requirements **133**

**W** Websites and internet access **134**

**Y** Youth hostels **134**

# A

## ACCESSIBLE TRAVEL

Porto's stone cobbles and steep hills don't make it easy for disabled travellers, but several of the main attractions are accessible. Most of the metro is accessible, as are some buses, but trams are inaccessible. Taxis are often the best option – drivers tend to be helpful and friendly and the prices are low. Adapted & Senior Tours Portugal (www.adaptedtoursportugal.com) offers holidays catered to people with disabilities. For more information on accessible tourism in Portugal visit www.visitportugal.com/en/experiencias/turismo-acessivel.

## ACCOMMODATION

The most appealing places to stay are found in the city centre, while the newer, more bland hotels (many with business facilities) are further out of town, for example at Boavista. Here, you get more for your euros, but the sheer convenience of being based near the centre, in a city of hills, is worth a lot. The hotel scene has been burgeoning in recent years with the opening of dozens of new hotels, many of them upmarket or chic boutique hotels. The city has also seen a surge of Airbnbs, apartments and guesthouses. Prices are steadily increasing but Porto is still good value compared with most cities in western Europe.

In high season (June–September) rooms are at a premium and you should book well ahead. Spring and late autumn are busy periods too, but in mid-winter Porto is relatively peaceful and prices can fall substantially. Whatever time you visit, the best rates are usually secured by booking in advance. If you arrive on spec, head for one of the tourist offices (see page 130) who will help you find accommodation. The official tourist board website (www.visitportoandnorth. travel) features an accommodation section with hotels ranging from 5 to 2-star.

Many hotels charge extra for breakfast. Check when you make a reservation. Charges can be high (eg €18 per person in a 4-star hotel) and you may prefer to go to the local café for coffee and croissants at a fraction of the price.

Be prepared for the City Tourist Tax, introduced in 2018 for those staying overnight in the city. The charge is €2 per adult per night, subject to a maximum of seven nights, but not applicable to children under 14. The tax is not included in the rates advertised on hotel booking websites and is charged directly to guests at the hotel.

What's the rate per night? **Qual é o preço por noite?**

# AIRPORT

Porto's Aeroporto Francisco Sá Carneiro (www.ana.pt) is 17km (10.5 miles) north of the city centre. The easiest way to get to the centre of Porto is by Metro Purple Line E in the direction of Estádio do Dragão, changing at Casa da Música (which serves Boavista hotels) on to the yellow Trindade Line D for central hotels. The metro runs from 6am–1am, there are two or three trains an hour and the journey takes 25–35 minutes. The multi-option metro ticket machines can be a bit complex for first-timers but there is a good tourist office at the airport which sells tickets. Taxis to the centre cost €25–35, and there is a growing number of Uber cars in the city.

How much is it to downtown Porto? **Quanto custa para ir ao centro de Porto?**

# B

# BICYCLE HIRE

Given Porto's hilly terrain, uneven streets and traffic-filled lanes, few tourists choose to hire a bike, or if they do it's an electric one. However, there is easy biking along a cycle path all the way from the Dom Luís I bridge alongside the River Douro to the beaches of Foz do Douro and extending to Matosinhos.

Across the river in Vila Nova de Gaia you can also cycle beside the river, then south via the Reserva Natural Local do Estuário do Douro (nature reserve) to the beaches of Espinho. In Ribeira bikes can be rented from Porto Rent a Bike, Avenida Gustavo Eiffel No. 280 (www.portorentabike.com) on the waterfront, just beyond the Dom Luís I bridge. Electric, tandem and folding bikes are available, and accessories such as locks, maps, helmets and child seats are included in the price. A Dutch bike costs €10 for half a day, €15 for 24 hours, while e-bikes are €20 for half a day, €35 for 24 hours.

# BUDGETING FOR YOUR TRIP

**Accommodation.** A double room in a simple hotel or B&B costs €90–130, in the mid-range category from €130–180 and for a 4-star plus expect to pay over €200. Hostel accommodation is plentiful, with dorms for around €20 and double rooms from €40–75.

**Flights.** Flights from London airports start at around £80 return off season, with a low-cost carrier. Summer flights are more likely to be £200–300.

**Meals and drinks.** Eating out is more affordable than most European capitals, especially if you choose to have your main meal at lunchtime. A 3-course dinner with wine in a mid-range restaurant would cost around €35 or in an upmarket one from €45 upwards. Portions are often gargantuan and you can cut costs by sharing. Most restaurants offer a midday fixed-price meal, often no more than €10–15 for three courses. A coffee costs anything from 80 cents (espresso in a local bar) to €4 (cappuccino served in a smart bar or main square); local beer is €2–4, a bottle of wine in a restaurant €15–25, house wine in a carafe a good deal less.

**Museums.** Admission fees range from €2.50–10. Some museums are free on the first Sunday of the month, others (eg Serralves Museum of Contemporary Art and Soares dos Reis National Museum) are free on Sundays until 1pm.

The Porto Card includes free admission to 11 museums and a 50% discount on eight sights, plus an optional travel card for unlimited access to the metro, buses and urban trains. Cards are available online and at the airport (purchase it there to save on travel to the centre). The hour and date should be written on the back of your card when you first use it. A card without transport costs €6, €10, €13 and €15 for 1, 2, 3 and 4 days, passes with travel for the same periods are €13, €20, €25 and €33.

# C

## CAMPING

There is no camping in Porto itself and the nearest sites are a 50–60-minute bus journey away from the city centre. The chain Orbitur (www.orbitur.pt) has two sites, Orbitur Angeiras 16km north of Porto at the seaside village of Angeiras, and Orbitur Madalena, close to Madalena beach, 8km from the centre of Vila Nova de Gaia. Campsites tend to be very crowded and noisy in summer.

## CAR HIRE

Major international companies such as Avis, Hertz and Europcar have offices both at the airport and in Porto, but for the best deals book online in advance. Local companies include Auto-Jardim and Bluealliance. Car rental costs from around €150 per week for a small car. The minimum age of hiring a car is 21–25 (depending on the company) and anyone hiring must have held a valid licence for at least one year. Rental companies will accept your home country's national driving license but you must show your passport. Third-party insurance should be included in the basic charge. Optional excess insurance costs from around €15 a day; it is far cheaper to take out your own excess insurance policy in advance.

## CLIMATE

July and August are the hottest months, although there are rarely heat waves. June, September and October are warm, pleasant and less crowded. Porto is

I'd like to rent a car for one day/week **Queria alugar um carro por um dia/uma semana** well north of Lisbon and has far more rain. The wettest months are October to January, but April can be wet too and late spring can be surprisingly cool. Winter is the quietest (and coldest) season, with some great hotel discounts. In the Douro Valley the summers are stifling and should be avoided. If you want to witness (or even join in) the grape harvest, go from mid- to late September, but for the colours of the foliage wait until late October or early November.

|   | J | F | M | A | M | J | J | A | S | O | N | D |
|---|---|---|---|---|---|---|---|---|---|---|---|---|
| C | 10 | 11 | 12 | 13 | 15 | 18 | 20 | 20 | 19 | 16 | 13 | 12 |
| F | 50 | 52 | 54 | 55 | 59 | 64 | 68 | 68 | 66 | 61 | 55 | 54 |

## CLOTHING

Apart from the mid-summer months, when all you need is light, cool clothes and perhaps a wrap, bring plenty of layers, an umbrella and raincoat and in winter a warm coat. Comfortable walking shoes are essential for the steep cobbled streets. When visiting churches cover shoulders and don't wear skimpy attire.

## CRIME AND SAFETY

Crime levels are low in Porto, but it is sensible to take precautions as you would in any city. In busy places, beware of pickpockets –some of them don smart attire to avoid suspicion. Leave important documents and valuables in the hotel safe and keep a firm hold of handbags, especially in crowded public areas and on public transport. For insurance purposes theft and loss must be reported immediately to the police (see Emergencies).

# D

## DRIVING

Avoid driving in the city centre if at all possible. Roads are congested and parking expensive. Most visitors cover Porto on foot, or use buses, trams, the metro or the affordable taxis and Ubers. Few tourists find it necessary to hire a car to see the region, but driving is one of the best ways of seeing the Douro Valley (see page 82).

To bring your own car into Portugal you will need your national driving licence, registration papers and insurance. The main roads are generally in good repair.

**Rules and regulations.** The rules of the road are the same as in most western European countries. Drive on the right. At roundabouts the vehicle already on the roundabout has priority, unless road markings or lights indicate otherwise. Seat belts are compulsory and a heavy fine can be imposed for not wearing one. Speed limits are 120km/h (75mph) on motorways, 100km/h (62.5mph) on roads restricted to motor vehicles, 90km/h (56mph) on other roads and 50km/h (37mph) in urban areas.

**Breakdowns.** Dial 112 for an operator to connect you to an emergency service. Operators can answer your call in English.

# E

## ELECTRICITY
220V/50Hz is standard. Sockets take two-pin, round pronged plugs. Visitors from the UK and the US will require an adaptor or transformer.

## EMBASSIES AND CONSULATES
**Australia** Avenida da Liberdade 200, 2nd floor, Lisbon, tel: (+351) 213 101 500; www.portugal.embassy.gov.au

---

Are we on the right road for...? **É esta estrada para...?**
Fill the tank, please **Encha o depósito faz favor**
My car's broken down **O meu carro está avariado**
There's been an accident **Houve um acidente**

**Canada** Avenida da Liberdade 198-200, 3rd floor, Lisbon, tel: (+351) 213 164 600; www.canadainternational.gc.ca/portugal

**Ireland** Avenida da Liberdade 200, 4th floor, Lisbon, tel: (+351) 213 308 200; www.dfa.ie/irish-embassy/portugal

**New Zealand** Rua de Sociedade Farmacêutica 68, Lisbon, tel: (+351) 213 140 780; https://www.mfat.govt.nz

**South Africa** Avenida Luís Bivar 10, Lisbon, tel: (+351) 213 192 200; www.embaixada-africadosul.pt

**UK** Rua de São Bernardo 33, Lisbon, tel: (+351) 213 924 000; https://www.gov.uk/world/organisations/british-embassy-lisbon

**US** Avenida das Forças Armadas 16, Lisbon, tel: (+351) 217 273 300; www.pt.usembassy.gov

Where's the British/American embassy? **Onde é a embaixada inglesa/americana?**

## EMERGENCIES
General emergency, 24 hours a day: 112

# G

## GETTING THERE

**By air.** Porto is linked by daily direct flights with many European cities. Portugal's flag carrier airline, TAP Air Portugal (www.flytap.com) and British Airways (www.ba.com) operate scheduled flights between London and Porto. The city is also well served by low-cost UK carriers including Ryanair (www.ryanair.com) and easyJet (www.easyjet.com).

TAP Air Portugal and United Airlines (www.united.com) both operate direct services to Porto from New York; Air Transat (www.airtransat.com) and Air Canada (www.aircanada.com) fly direct from Toronto to Porto.

**By sea.** Cruise ships dock at Leixões, about 10km from the centre of Porto. Brittany Ferries (www.brittany-ferries.co.uk) has crossings from Portsmouth, UK, to Santander and Bilbao in Spain and from Plymouth to Santander. The drive from northern Spain to Porto is then likely to take another 6–7 hours.

**By rail.** Portugal is linked to the European railway network and connections to Porto are possible from various points throughout Spain, France and the rest of continental Europe. The Portuguese national railway network is called CP (Comboios de Portugal, www.cp.pt). The main railway station in Porto is Campanhã, which is where international, national and regional train services arrive. From here there are regular connections to the central city station of São Bento.

**By car.** Major motorways connect Portugal with Spain at numerous border points. The drive from London to Porto via France and Spain takes 21–23 hours (1,259 miles/2026km). Porto and Lisbon are linked by the A1, with a journey time of around three hours. France, Spain and Portugal all charge highway tolls.

# GUIDES AND TOURS

Information on tours is available at tourist offices or from your hotel. River trips depart from the quaysides on both sides of the River Douro. Several different companies offer the hour-long, scenic Six Bridges cruise (€12–15 per person), some offering the option of combining it with a visit to port wine cellars. Living Tours (www.livingtours.com) offers a wide choice of well-run guided tours in Porto and beyond, including Douro Valley cruises.

Sign up for a free tour with Porto Walkers (www.portowalkers.pt) to explore the city on foot with a local guide and group of like-minded travellers. These are easy-going, friendly tours for all ages, and you can pick from different themes – history, wine, food, lifestyle – to best suit your interests. Dedicated foodies should look no further than Taste Porto Food and Wine Tours (www.tasteporto.com).

Various companies offer hop-on, hop-off bus tours with open-top buses and in season a tourist train loops around the centre and crosses the river for a stop at Vila Nova de Gaia.

We'd like an English-speaking guide **Queremos um guia que fale inglês**

# H

## HEALTH AND MEDICAL CARE

Standards of hygiene in Porto and in Portugal as a whole are generally very high; the most likely illness to befall travellers will be the result of an excess of sun or alcohol. The water is safe to drink. Farmácias (chemists/drugstores) are open during normal business hours, and one shop in each neighbourhood is on duty around the clock. Addresses can be found on pharmacy doors or in the daily paper, *Jornal de Notícias*.

The main hospital in Porto is the Hospital Santo António, Largo do Prof Abel Salazar, tel: 222 077 500, open 24 hours. In the event of an accident or sudden illness, call 112. There is no charge and the number is accessible from anywhere in the country at any time of day.

Hospital treatment is free to citizens of EU countries on production of a European Health Insurance Card (EHIC). UK citizens are entitled to free emergency treatment at Social Security and municipal hospitals in Portugal on production of a GHIC (Global Health Insurance Card, available online at Ⓦ nhs. uk). UK citizens in possession of a EHIC can continue to use the card until its expiry date, at which point they should obtain a GHIC. Privately billed hospital

Where's the nearest (all night) pharmacy? **Onde fica a farmácia (de serviço) mais próxima?**
I need a doctor/dentist **Preciso de um médico/dentista**
an ambulance **uma ambulância**

visits are expensive. Check your medical insurance to be sure it covers illness or accident while you are abroad. Nationals of other countries should check whether their government has a reciprocal health agreement, and/or ensure that they have adequate insurance cover.

At the time of writing, travellers to Portugal are not required to present a Covid-19 vaccination certificate nor a PCR/lateral flow test result. However, travel restrictions can change with no prior warning; check the latest entry requirements before you fly.

# L

## LANGUAGE

Portuguese is the sixth most spoken language in the world, with around 220 million native speakers and 260 million total speakers. It is spoken in Brazil, Angola, Mozambique and Macau – all former colonies of Portugal. Any school Spanish may help with signs and menus, but will not unlock the mysteries of spoken Portuguese with its many nasal sounds.

Virtually all hotels have staff who speak English and unless you go off the beaten track you should have little problem communicating in shops or restaurants. Most menus are translated into English; if not waiters will assist. Older taxi drivers may not speak English, but if you write down the destination this should not be a problem.

Almost everyone understands Spanish and many speak French, particularly the older generation, but just learning a few simple phrases in Portuguese will certainly enhance your visit and help if you are off the tourist circuit.

## LGBTQ+ TRAVELLERS

Porto is becoming one of the most popular LGBTQ+ destinations in Europe. It may be a little more conservative than Amsterdam or Berlin, but attitudes are generally relaxed and you will see plenty of same-sex couples wandering the city streets. The Porto Pride party held here in July each year first took place in 2001. Now the city also hosts the Porto International Queer Film Festival in October.

For local information on gay life in Porto visit www.portogaycircuit.com. Bars and clubs catering for an LGBTQ+ crowd are plentiful. Popular LGBTQ+ venues in the city include *Pride Café* (Praça Marquês de Pombal 13), a gay café by day and dancefloor by night, *Zoom Nightclub* (Rua de Passos Manuel 40, Fri and Sat only) and *Invictus* (Rua da Conceição 8/9), a small café-bar with drag shows.

# M

## MAPS

Tourist information offices and hotels provide complimentary maps of Porto and the surrounding area, though it is often hard to find one with all the small streets marked.

## MEDIA

Europe's principal newspapers, including most British dailies, are available on the day of publication. The weekly *Portugal News* (www.theportugalnews.com), published in the Algarve, is the country's main English-language paper and covers news and stories from around the country.

Free Portuguese/English booklets include *Lisboa Convida* (also online at www.lisboa.convida.pt), a six-monthly shopping and leisure guide, available from tourist offices and some hotels. Many but by no means all hotels have TVs with English-language channels such as BBC News and CNN. Foreign films are usually shown in the original language with subtitles.

---

Can I pay with a credit card? **Posso pagar com cartão de crédito?**
How much is that? **Quanto custa isto?**
Where's the nearest bank/currency exchange office? **Onde fica o banco mais próximo/a casa de câmbio mais próxima?**

## MONEY MATTERS

**Currency.** In common with most other European countries, the official currency used in Portugal is the euro (€), divided into 100 cents. Euro notes come in denominations of 500, 200, 100, 50, 20, 10 and 5; coins come in denominations of 2 and 1, then 50, 20, 10, 5, 2 and 1 cents.

**Credit cards and cash machines.** MasterCard and Visa are the most widely accepted credit cards. Many places don't accept American Express. Some small shops and restaurants are cash only, or take credit cards only for purchases of more than €10. You also need to have cash handy for museums and nightclubs. Cash machines are widespread. You can take out a maximum of €200 a day.

**Exchange facilities.** Banks offer the best rates, followed by exchange offices and hotels. Some exchange offices offer commission-free facilities, but check that the exchange rate is not exorbitant.

**O**

## OPENING HOURS

Banks open Mon–Fri 8.30am–3pm. Shops open Mon–Sat 9.30/10am–7/7.30pm, although some have shorter opening hours on Saturday and some of the smaller shops close for lunch. An increasing number of outlets are now open on Sundays, including shopping centres outside the city centre. Many shops and galleries in the Bombarda district don't open until noon, closing at 7 or 8pm.

Most museums are closed on Monday and public holidays.

Where's the nearest police station? **Onde fica o posto de polícia mais próximo?**
I've lost my ...wallet/bag/passport **Perdi...a minha carteira/o meu saco/o meu passaporte**

# P

## POLICE

The Portuguese national police, identified by their blue uniforms, are generally helpful and often speak a little English. On the roads, traffic is controlled by the Guarda Nacional Republicana (GNR). Occasionally police make spot-checks on documents or tyres and can issue on-the-spot fines, payable in cash only.

The multilingual Tourist Police are at Rua Clube dos Fenianos 11 (tel: 222 081 833; daily 8am–2am) beside the main tourist office.

The general emergency number is 112.

## POST OFFICES

Post offices (*correios*) are normally open Mon–Fri 9am–6pm but the main post office, the Posto de Correios dos Aliados on Praça General Humberto Delgado, has longer hours: Mon–Fri 8.30am–9pm, Sat 9am–6pm.

Where's the nearest post office? **Onde fica a estação de correios mais próxima?**

## PUBLIC HOLIDAYS

**1 January** *Ano Novo* New Year's Day
**25 April** *Dia da Liberdade* 1974 Revolution Day
**1 May** *Dia do Trabalhador* May Day
**10 June** *Dia de Portugal* or *Dia de Camões* National Day
**24 June** *São João* (Porto only)
**15 August** *Assunção* The Assumption
**5 October** *Implantação da República* Republic Day
**1 November** *Todos-os-Santos* All Saints' Day

**1 December** *Dia da Independência* Independence Day
**8 December** *Imaculada Conceição* Immaculate Conception
**25 December** *Natal* Christmas Day
Moveable dates:
*Sexta-feira Santa* Good Friday
*Corpo de Deus* Corpus Christi

# R

## RELIGION

The Portuguese are predominantly Roman Catholic, a fact reflected in surviving religious rituals and saints' days that are public holidays. However only a small percentage regularly attend Mass. The St James Anglican Church Porto on Largo da Maternidade de Julio Dinis (www.stjamesoporto.org) holds services on Sundays and Thursdays.

# T

## TELEPHONES

Portugal's country code is 351. The local area code for Porto is 22 and must be dialled before all phone numbers, including local calls. To make an international call, dial 00 followed by the country code (UK 44, Australia 61, Canada and the US 1), plus the phone number including the area code, but without the initial '0' where there is one.

**Mobile (cell) phones.** Check the international roaming rates with your provider prior to departure. In mid-2017 roaming charges within the EU were abolished but have been reintroduced for UK citizens post-Brexit. Roaming

| New York | London | **Porto** | Paris | Sydney | Auckland |
|----------|--------|-----------|-------|--------|----------|
| 7am | noon | **noon** | 1pm | 9pm | 11pm |

charges can be quite high for non-EU countries and if you are making a lot of calls or staying for some time it may be worth purchasing a SIM 'pay as you go' card available at shops of the main providers or at the post office.

## TIME ZONES

Portugal, being at the western edge of Europe, maintains Greenwich Mean Time (GMT), along with the UK, and is therefore one hour behind the rest of the EU. From the last Sunday in March until the last Sunday in October the clocks are moved one hour ahead for summer time, GMT + 1.

## TIPPING

Tipping isn't mandatory or expected in Porto. Bear in mind, however, that wages for service staff are low so anything you can spare is appreciated. Service is not usually added to restaurant bills and a tip of 10 percent is normal, provided you think the service warrants it. Hotel porters generally receive a euro for each bag they carry; taxi drivers don't necessarily expect a tip but are grateful if you round the fare up.

## TOILETS

Public toilets are hard to come by, but you can find them in stations, museums and large shops. Otherwise it is generally a case of using the facilities of a café or bar. Toilets are marked *Senhoras* (ladies) and *Homens* (men).

Where are the toilets? **Onde é o lavabo/quarto de banho?**

## TOURIST INFORMATION

Tourist offices can provide a free city map, list of opening hours for city sights and a programme of current events. The main tourist office **Turismo Sé** is located at Terreiro da Sé, occupying the medieval tower opposite the Cathedral, tel: 223 393 472 (same opening hours).

Other tourist offices and information offices:

Porto's **Francisco Sá Carneiro airport** has a good tourist office in the Arrivals Hall.

**iPoint Aliados**, green kiosk on Praça da Liberdade (May–Oct daily 9.30am–6.30pm, Nov–Apr weather permitting Mon–Fri 9.30am–7pm).

**iPoint Campanhã**, inside Campanhã railway station (daily June–Aug 9.30am–6.30pm with one hour break).

**iPoint Ribeira** Praça da Ribeira (daily May–Sept 10.30am–7pm, Oct 10.30am–6pm).

**Vila Nova de Gaia Turismo** on the waterfront at Avenida Diogo Leite 135, tel: 223 758 288 (Apr–Sept daily 10am–6pm, Oct–Mar Mon–Sat 10am–6pm).

# TRANSPORT

## Metro

Porto has a swish modern metro system (www.metrodoporto.pt) operating six easy-to-use lines, A to F. Trains run from 6am–1am, and arrive every 4–15 minutes. The network is limited and for visitors the most useful routes are Line E (Purple) between the airport and the centre, Line A (Blue) linking Porto to Matosinhos and Line B (Red) to the seaside resort of Vila do Conde. All lines converge at the Trindade stop, just north of Avenida dos Aliados. For getting around the centre you are better off going by foot, bus or tram, though the Casa da Música metro stop is useful if you are staying in Boavista or visiting the concert hall or Serralves. Currently in progress is a new Line G (Pink), which will link Casa da Música and São Bento via Plaza de Galicia and Hospital de Santo António when it opens in 2023/24.

Rechargeable Andante cards can be used for the metro, buses and some suburban trains. (Trams, funiculars, boats and cable-car have different tickets and prices.) The card cost is €0.60 and is available from ticket machines, Andante shops (eg in the airport and metro stations) and also from railway stations, tourist offices and some hotels. The card can be credited for single journeys, 10 tickets or 24-hour travel. The price depends on which of the three zones (Z2, Z3 and Z4) you travel to. Zone 2 is sufficient for getting around central Porto but the airport is in Zone 4. One trip for Zone 2 costs €1.20, for

Zone 4 it is €2. Transfers can be made within one hour with the same ticket. If you change metro lines you have to swipe your card again. One- and three-day travel cards with unlimited travel on the metro, buses and locals trains are available. Cards are activated when first used and must be validated on each journey. The metro is open from 6am–1am.

> Where can I get a taxi? **Onde posso encontrar um táxi?**
> What's the fare to...? **Quanto custa um bilhete para...?**
> Where is the nearest bus stop? **Onde é a paragem de autocarros mais próxima?**
> I want a ticket to... **Queria um bilhete para...**
> single/return **ida/ida e volta**
> Will you tell me when to get off? **Pode dizer-me quando devo descer?**

**Trains**

Trains are run by CP (Comboios de Portugal, www.cp.pt). The main railway station in Porto is the Estação de Campanhã, on the east edge of town, where international and national trains on longer routes (eg from Lisbon) arrive. From Campanhã station there are constant connections to the Estação de São Bento, the central railway station used for most of the regional and inter-regional services. Both Campanhã and São Bento have metro stations. Timetables and fares are available on the CP website. Discounts on train journeys are available for those with a student card or who are under 26.

**Bus and tram**

Porto has an extensive bus system operated by STCP (www.stcp.pt). Main hubs are Jardim da Cordoaria, Praça Almeida Garrett and Praça da Liberdade. You can buy a ticket on board or use an Andante card (see page 131). Tickets must be validated in the machine on the bus. Information on fares and timetables is available on the STCP website. Buses usually operate between

6am and midnight or 1am. The most scenic route is bus #500, which links the centre of Porto to Foz do Douro.

The appealing vintage trams (carros eléctricos) only operate on three routes, the most popular (and crowded) being #1, which runs from the historic centre of Porto along the riverside to the coast. Trams are not covered by the Andante card. Tickets (€3.50 per journey) can be bought from the driver. The trams are hugely popular with tourists but locals tend to take the faster and cheaper buses. Tram times vary according to the time of year.

**Funiculars**

The useful Funicular dos Guindais connects the Ribeira, at the foot of the Dom Luís I bridge, with the city centre, climbing a steep hill to Rua da Batalha. Funiculars run every 10 minutes and tickets cost €2.50 each way. At Vila Nova de Gaia the panoramic Teleférico de Gaia cable car (www.gaiacablecar.com) climbs from the riverfront up to the Jardim do Morro. It's a pricey 5 minute ride (€6 one way, €9 return) but affords fine views of the wine lodges and city of Porto.

**Taxis and tuk-tuks**

Taxis in Porto are cheap by European standards. The cars are beige or black with a green roof. Taxi ranks can be found at main squares and stations but can also be hailed in the street. The fare is shown on the meter – check that it's running before you set off. There are extra charges at night and at weekends, and for luggage placed in the boot. For a radio taxi call Táxis Invicta (tel: 225 076 400) or Raditáxis (tel: 225 073 900). Uber works well in Porto and the fares are a good deal cheaper than those of normal taxis. Drivers normally turn up promptly. Water taxis link the waterfront at Ribeira with Vila Nova de Gaia opposite (€3 one way). Tuk-tuks, seating up to three, can be found at the most popular sights. Guided tours cost €15–65 depending on the length of the journey.

# V

---

# VISAS AND ENTRY REQUIREMENTS

For UK and EU citizens, a valid passport or identity card is all that is needed to enter Portugal for stays of up to 90 days. Citizens of Australia, Canada, New

Zealand and the US require only a valid passport. For stays of more than 90 days a visa or residence permit is required.

# W

## WEBSITES AND INTERNET ACCESS

www.visitportoandnorth.travel Official tourist website for Porto and northern Portugal

www.visitportugal.com The official Portuguese tourism site

www.flytap.com TAP/Air Portugal, the national airline

www.cp.pt Comboios de Portugal, the railway network

Free wi-fi can be found in most cafés, bars, restaurants and hotels.

# Y

## YOUTH HOSTELS

Porto now has dozens of youth hostels spread around the city, ranging from very basic to luxury, with en suite double rooms. Some of the hostels organise activities such as free walks, theme nights and parties. Breakfast is often included in the room rate. At the very top of the list is the comfortable, art-themed *Hostel Porto Gallery* (see page 140). The centrally located *Poets' Inn* (Rua dos Caldeireiros 261, tel: 223 324 209, www.thepoetsinn.com), close to the Clérigos Tower, is newly furnished and tastefully decorated, while the *Passenger Hostel* (tel: 963 802 000, www.thepassengerhostel.com) is located right inside Estação São Bento and comes with excellent facilities, stylish interiors and a buzzy vibe.

# WHERE TO STAY

Porto offers accommodation to suit all tastes: five-star big-hitters, boutique hotels, unassuming guesthouses, hostels, apartments and Airbnbs. There's even a castle you can stay in. In high season (June to September) rooms are at a premium and you should book well ahead. The rates can change significantly with demand and facilities. Best rates are normally those booked through a hotel's own website, and discounts are sometimes available for stays of longer than three nights. Short-term rentals are becoming increasingly popular, but expect a minimum night stay.

The price indication is for a double room in high season including breakfast, service and VAT, but excluding the tourist tax, which is €2 per person, per night for visitors aged 14 and over (see page 116). All the hotels take major credit cards unless otherwise stated.

| | |
|---|---|
| €€€€ | **over 250 euros** |
| €€€ | **180–250 euros** |
| €€ | **120–180 euros** |
| € | **under 120 euros** |

## RIBEIRA

**1872 River House €€€** *Rua do Infante D. Henrique*; www.1872riverhouse. com. A little gem of a hotel converted from a pastel pink riverside townhouse. Just eight individually furnished rooms create an intimate and exclusive feel, each with views of the city or river. Guests are very well looked after, with excellent breakfasts (highlights include the freshly made pastries and eggs to order) and welcoming, helpful staff. Tea, coffee, snacks and (unusually) beer are available all day.

**Da Bolsa €€** *Rua Ferreira Borges 101*; www.hoteldabolsa.com. No-frills, three-star hotel with a prime location in the heart of Porto. The building started life in 1908 as a private social club, then became the HQ of an insurance company before its new lease of life as a guesthouse. It is clean and comfortable with helpful staff, though rooms are a tad old-fashioned.

**Guest House Douro €€–€€€** *Rua Fonte Taurina 99–101*; www.guesthouse-douro.com. This was the first guesthouse on the Ribeira waterfront. A brave young couple, Carmen and João, bought and restored the house several years ago when Porto was rough around the edges and the city saw few tourists. Their intuition and leap of faith paid off: their stylish digs are now very much in demand, with four of the eight rooms looking out directly over the River Douro.

**Hotel Neya Porto €** *Rua de Monchique 35–41*; www.porto.neyahotels.com. Opened in 2022, *Hotel Neya* is a smart bolthole set in a converted porcelain warehouse and parts of an old convent. Rooms are cool and contemporary, with floor-to-ceiling windows framing views of the river, gardens or original cloisters. There's a rooftop bar, a Portuguese fine-dining restaurant encased in glass for fine Douro views, and a small spa for massages. Ribeira Square is a 15min walk away, or 5min by bus or tram, with transport links outside the hotel. It's on a fairly busy road, but excellent soundproofing ensures a good night's sleep.

**Infante Sagres €€€€** *Praça D. Filipa de Lencastre 62*; www.infantesagres.com. The grande dame of Porto's hotels reopened in 2018 after a major renovation. Among its roster of VIP guests are the Dalai Lama and Bob Dylan as well as European royalty and presidents. Old-word elegance predominates, though new additions such as the Vogue Café with 'Food for the Fashionable' have added a touch of twenty-first-century glamour.

**InPátio Guest House €** *Pátio de São Salvador 22*; www.inpatio.pt. This is a centrally located but quiet B&B with a clutch of comfortable guest rooms. Owners Fernando and Olga extend a warm welcome and are happy to offer local tips and help organize your travel itinerary. Excellent breakfasts, with home-made bread and warm-from-the-oven cake.

**Pestana Vintage Port Hotel €€€€** *Praça da Ribeira 1*; www.pestana.com. A conversion of a group of old riverside houses, this pricey boutique hotel in the Pestana group has a prime location in the heart of Ribeira. Guest rooms are sleek and modern, but vary in shape and size. Many have superb views of the Dom Luís I bridge and river. Good half-board deals with lunch or dinner in the *Rib Beef and Wine Restaurant*.

**Port River Apartments €€€** *Rua dos Canastreiros 50*; www.portoriver.pt. In a historic building in Ribeira, this aparthotel is a stylish fusion of old and new. Rooms have rough stone walls, wood floors, exposed beams, contemporary furnishings and well-equipped kitchenettes. The pick of the bunch have views of the River Douro.

# BAIXA (DOWNTOWN)

**A.S.1829 €€** *Largo de São Domingos 45–55*; www.artsoulgroup.com/portoas1829hotel. The A.S. stands for Aranjo e Sobinho: the paper warehouse, print business and stationery shop (dating from 1829) that once occupied the building. Look out for the discreet nods to its heritage, from old typewriters to vintage fountain pens and original typography designs. The hotel has a great location, just a short walk up from Ribeira. The guest rooms are stylish, cool and contemporary, with good soundproofing, and there is a great choice of restaurants within a stone's throw. The hotel's own *Galeria do Largo* restaurant, overlooking the square, serves traditional Portuguese dishes.

**Cale Guest House €** *Largo de São Domingos 28; tel: 966 686 081*. Popular little guesthouse in a perfect location, just a couple of minutes up from the waterfront. The seven newly furnished rooms have white walls, wood floors, mid-century furniture and a balcony or patio. Good breakfasts too.

**Casa dos Lóios €€** *Rua das Flores 245*; www.shiadu.com/en/cities/porto-en. A charming and quirky guesthouse in an excellent location on the lovely Rua das Flores with reasonable prices. It occupies part of a restored sixteenth--century house and preserves some of the original architectural features. Interiors are peppered with antique one-offs and cool artwork, while a small terrace is adorned with huge terracotta pots. The staff are exceptionally helpful, the breakfasts are good and there is complimentary tea, coffee and cake.

**Castelo de Santa Catarina €€** *Rua de Santa Catarina 1347*; www.castelosantacatarina.com. If you don't mind being a little out of the centre, you can stay in a turreted castle surrounded by verdant gardens. It dates from 1887 and was a private home before being converted into a hotel. Accommodation is either in traditional rooms with period furnishings within the castle (note: no lift) or modern ones in the new wing.

**Dom Henrique €€€** *Rua Guedes de Azevedo 179*; www.hoteldomhenrique.pt. This high-rise hotel north of the centre is geared to business travellers, but is also popular with tourists for its reasonable prices, spacious comfortable rooms, four-star amenities and seventeenth-floor panoramic restaurant.

**The Editory Artist Hotel €€** *Rua da Firmeza 49*; www.editoryhotels.com/artist-baixa-porto. A 5min walk uphill from Porto's main shopping artery, Rua de Santa Catarina, this 17-room bolthole is managed by students from the local hospitality school. In a nod to its roots as a former schools of arts, the hotel is adorned with a rich tapestry of artwork, sculpture and photography by past students. It's a riot of colour and texture – blood-orange armchairs, teal cushions, mustard-hued sofas. There's an excellent restaurant (opt for the nightly degustation menu for high-quality food at bargain prices), an inviting bar and a lovely outdoor courtyard which hosts live music and events in the summer.

**Grande Hotel de Paris €€** *Rua da Fábrica 27*; www.stayhotels.pt/grandehotelparis. A building long associated with music and literature, this became a hotel under French owners in 1877. 'Grand' is a tad misleading, but it has old-world charm, with small salons for reading and a fine breakfast room overlooking a garden of lemon trees and bird-of-paradise plants. Bedrooms and bathrooms could do with an update but, given the location, the prices are good.

**InterContinental Porto €€€€** *Praça da Liberdade 25*; www.ihg.com. The historic Palácio das Cardosas, once the site of a monastery, now offers five-star luxury and impeccable service under its *InterContinental* guise. Right in the city centre, it stands conspicuously at the southern end of the main Avenida dos Aliados, within easy walking distance of all the main sights. A discretely grand facade conceals plush and palatial interiors with large chandeliers, marble floors and a gallery of exclusive shops. Guests can enjoy fine dining and expert wine pairing in the *Astoria* restaurant, and tea, cocktails and live-music in the elegant library-style *Bar das Cardosas*.

**M Maison Particulière €€€** *Largo de São Domingos 66*; www.m-porto.com. Exclusive, French-inspired boutique hotel helmed by a mother-and-son team. The beautifully restored sixteenth-century house preserves stuccowork, wood-carved ceilings and original fireplaces. There are 10 individually designed suites, decorated with original antiques, luxury fabrics in jewel tones and lithographs by modern artists. Pick Room 9 for a private balcony overlooking the city with views stretching to the port wine cellars of Gaia. The location couldn't be better, just 500yds from the São Bento train station and close to the Ribeira waterfront, with excellent restaurants all around.

**The Passenger Hostel €** *Estação S.Bento*; www.thepassengerhostel.com. You don't have to stray far from the train station if you're bedding down at *The Passenger*: this hostel is located inside São Bento. Interiors are stylish, with vintage finds and cool local artworks (which you can buy), plus a drive for sustainability (it's won the Green Key three years running). Facilities are excellent: a lively bar with local ales and Porto wine; two living rooms with low-slung sofas, a smart TV and Bose sound system; a fully equipped kitchen and dining space; and an interior 'garden' with a bar, suspended sofas and beer pong. There's a 10-person mixed dorm and private rooms sleeping 2-4 (all with shared bathrooms), plus a suite sleeping 5 guests (private bathroom).

**Poets' Inn €** *Rua dos Caldeireiros 261*; www.thepoetsinn.com. This hostel is tucked down a quiet street, within walking distance of major landmarks (Torre dos Clérigos is just steps away) and plentiful restaurants. It offers imaginatively decorated rooms with shared bathrooms and a well-equipped kitchen.

**PortoBay Flores €€** *Rua das Flores 27*; www.portobay.com. A sixteenth-century palace has been transformed into this gorgeous hotel, with its traditional Portuguese tiles, wrought-iron balconies and original granite flooring. There are 66 rooms – 55 in the new building and 11 in the old mansion. Ask for a top-floor abode for serene views of the city's terracotta roofs.

**PortoBay Teatro €€** *Rua Sá da Bandiera 84*; www.portobay.com. On the site of Porto's old Baquet Theatre, the hotel is bright and airy after a 2021 renovation. The 74 rooms are decked out in a soothing palette of creams and golds, while the attractive *Il Basilico* restaurant serves Italian comfort food.

**São Domingos Oporto Tourist Apartments €€** *Largo São Domingos 86*; www.oportotouristapartments.com. Attractive contemporary apartments in an old building with high ceilings, wood floors and shutters. The location is perfect, just up from the Ribeira waterfront, and with such a good choice of neighbouring restaurants you may find the kichenette is superfluous.

**Torel 1884 €€** *Rua Mouzinho da Silveira 228*; www.torel1884.com. Housed in an elegant nineteenth-century palace, *Torel 1884* has retained the grandeur of the building: high ceilings, original staircase, crowning skylight. The 12-room hotel pays homage to Portuguese art and design, from the handcrafted chalky-white espresso cups at breakfast to the sculptures by João Pedro Rodrigues in the entrance hall. Ask for one of the rooms at the back as the front-facing rooms can get noisy.

## MIRAGAIA AND MASSARELOS

**Gallery Hostel Porto €** *Rua de Miguel Bombarda 222*; www.gallery-hostel.com. This hip hostel is ideal for art-lovers, occupying a 1906 townhouse hung with original artworks and located in the happening Bombarda arts quarter. En-suite dormitories, double rooms and suites are all Scandi minimalism in style; elsewhere, there's a summer terrace, winter garden, changing art exhibitions and nightly Portuguese dinners. Free walking tours, breakfast and wi-fi, very friendly staff too. No wonder it's popular.

**Pensão Favorita €** *Rua de Miguel Bombarda 267*; www.pensaofavorita.pt. Charming guesthouse with a pretty and unexpected garden. There are seven rooms in the main house, five in the garden, in contemporary and vintage style, all with private bathroom. Very welcoming, and good buffet breakfasts.

**Rosa et Al €€€** *Rua do Rosário 233*; www.rosaetal.pt. Close to the hip Bombarda quarter, this exclusive and much sought-after boutique hotel is set in a converted townhouse. As well as stylish rooms and a particularly good brunch, there are cookery classes twice a week (book ahead), knitting and mindfulness retreats, a coffee shop, concept store and in-room spa service.

**Torel Avantgarde €€€** *Rua da Restauração 336*; www.torelavantgarde.com. This five-star hotel is one of the hottest addresses in town. An art-lover's haven, it has 27 rooms and 20 suites named after famous avant-garde artists, writers, sculptors, architects and fashion designers, with decor reflecting the artist's personality and vision. Perched on the hillside, it has a small infinity pool and breathtaking views across the river to the wine lodges on the left bank. Confusingly, rooms come in 10 categories with wildly different prices, but all offering absolute comfort. The *Digby* restaurant, named after the English diplomat and philosopher who is known to have invented the modern wine bottle, offers contemporary Portuguese cuisine.

## BOAVISTA

**Hotel da Música €€** *Mercado do Bom Sucesso, Largo Ferreira Lapa*; www.hoteldamusica.com. Part of the revamped Mercado do Bom Sucesso, this four-star design-led hotel is an obvious choice for music-lovers, close to the Casa da Música and with a musical theme throughout. It's also good for gourmets, with all the culinary delights of the Mercado do Bom Sucesso on the doorstep. You can choose products from the market and have them cooked by the hotel's chef. It's a popular business hotel with reasonable prices but quite far from the centre.

## VILA NOVA DE GAIA

**Yeatman €€€€** *Rua do Choupelo, Vila Nova de Gaia*; www.the-yeatma-hotel.com. Poised above the Douro overlooking Porto's historic core, this five-star big-hitter is all about the luxury. Think glorious river views, two-Michelin-starred cuisine and second-to-none service. You can also expect fine port: the hotel is owned by the Taylor, Fladgate & Yeatman group, of the city's most prestigious producers of the tipple. And you aren't likely to forget it either, from the decanter-shaped pool and spa therapies using vine extracts to a 25,000-bottle cellar and even a wine museum at the onsite cultural village.

## FOZ DO DOURO

**Hotel Boa-Vista €€** *Esplanada do Castelo 58, Foz do Douro*; www.hotelboavista.com. Beach break meets city stay with a night at this traditional three-star bolthole in the suburb of Foz do Douro. Tram #1 and Bus #500 provide a good service along the waterfront into Porto. Built in 1900, the hotel lies across the road from the Fort of São João. Clean, comfortable rooms offer good value, and there are fine views of the River Douro where it meets the sea from the front rooms, top-floor restaurant, pool and terrace.

# INDEX

## A

accessible travel 116
accommodation 116
Afurada 80
airport 117
Alfândega Nova 53
Arabian Hall 32
Arts Block 56
Ascensor da Ribeira 28
Avenida dos Aliados 40

## B

Barredo 28, 38
bicycle hire 117
budgeting for your trip 118

## C

Café Majestic 42
Café Piolho 48
Cais da Ribeira 28
camping 119
Cantinho das Aromáticas 73
Capela de Santa Catarina 43
car hire 119
Casa da Música 61
Casa de Serralves 65
Casa do Infante 30
Casa-Museu Guerra Junqueiro 37
Castelo do Queijo 77
Cemitério de Agramonte 63
Centro Comercial Bombarda 57

Centro Português de Fotografia 48
Churchill's 69
Clérigos Complex 44
climate 119
Cloister 35
clothing 120
coffee 104, 106
crime and safety 120

## D

Dona Maria Pia Bridge 29
Douro and Port Wine Institute 33
Douro Valley 82
driving 120

## E

electricity 121
embassies and consulates 121
emergencies 122
Espaço Porto Cruz 69
Estação de São Bento 41

## F

Ferreira 69
Fort of São João da Foz 77
Foz do Douro 75
Foz do Douro and Matosinhos 75
Fundação Serralves 64
Funicular dos Guindais 30

## G

getting there 122

Graham's 68
greja de São Pedro de Miragaia 52
guides and tours 123

## H

Hard Club 31
health and medical care 124

## I

Igreja das Carmelitas and Igreja do Carmo 48
Igreja de Massarelos 59
Igreja de Santa Clara 38
Igreja de São Francisco 33
Igreja de São Ildefonso 41
Igreja dos Clérigos 45

## J

Jardim da Cordoaria 46
Jardim do Morro 71
Jardim do Palácio de Cristal 52, 57
Jardim do Passeio Alegre 76
Jewish quarter 50

## L

language 125
LGBTQ+ travellers 125
Livraria Lello 46

## M

maps 126
Market, cemetery and

synagogue 62
Matosinhos 78
media 126
Mercado de Bom Sucesso 62
Mercado de Matosinhos 80
Mercado do Bolhão 43
Mercado Ferreira Borges 31
Miradouro da Vitória 50
money matters 126
Mosteiro da Serra do Pilar 71
Murahla Fernandina 39
Museu da Igreja Misericórdia 50
Museu de Arte Contemporânea 64
Museu do Carro Eléctrico 59
Museu dos Transportes e Comunicações 53
Museu Nacional de Soares dos Reis 55
Museu Romântico 58

**O**
opening hours 127

**P**
Paço Episcopal 36
Palácio da Bolsa 32

Palácio de Cristal 57
Parque da Cidade 78
Passeio dos Clérigos 46
Pérgola da Foz 77
police 127
Ponte da Arrábida 60, 75
Ponte do Freizo 75
Ponte do Infante 74
Ponte Dom Luís I 29
Ponte Dona Maria Pia 74
Ponte São João 74
Port wine lodges 67
post offices 128
Praça da Batalha 41
Praça da Liberdade 40
Praça da Ribeira 28
Praça de Gomes Teixeira 47
public holidays 128

**R**
religion 129
Riverside Miragaia 52
Rua das Flores 50
Rua de Miguel Bombarda 56
Rua de Santa Caterina 42

**S**
Sea Life Porto 78
Serralves Park 65
Sinagoge Kadoorie 63

**T**
Taylor's 68
Teatro Nacional São João 41
Teleférico de Gaia 71
telephones 129
Terminal de Cruzeiros 78
Terreiro da Sé 36
the riverfront 70
The Sé 34
the waterfront 59
time zones 129
tipping 130
toilets 130
Torre dos Clérigos 44
tourist information 130
transport 131
Tree of Jesse 34

**V**
Vale do Douro 82
visas and entry requirements 133

**W**
websites and internet access 134
Wines of Portugal Tasting Rooms 33
World of Discoveries 54

**Y**
youth hostels 134

# THE **MINI** ROUGH GUIDE TO
# PORTO

**First Edition 2022**

**Editor:** Joanna Reeves
**Original author:** Susie Boulton
**Updater:** Joanna Reeves
**Picture Editor:** Tom Smyth
**Cartography Update:** Carte
**Layout:** Pradeep Thapliyal
**Head of DTP and Pre-Press:** Katie Bennett
**Head of Publishing:** Kate Drynan
**Photography Credits:** Coelho/Epa/REX/
Shutterstock 77; Daniel Rodrigues/Porto
Convention & Visitors Bureau 100; Getty Images
56, 84; iStock 23, 46, 49, 60; iStock 4MC, 4TC,
4ML, 4ML, 16, 29, 30, 33, 35, 36, 40, 45, 48, 51, 72,
74, 78, 81, 82, 104; Luis Ferraz/Porto Convention
& Visitors Bureau 64; Messias Delmar/Porto
Convention & Visitors Bureau 62; Porto
Convention & Visitors Bureau 19, 21, 63; Public
domain 22; Shutterstock 1, 4TC, 4MC, 4TL, 5T,
5M, 5M, 6T, 6B, 7T, 7B, 10, 12, 14, 26, 38, 43, 53, 54,
58, 65, 66, 69, 76, 79, 87, 88, 90, 92, 95, 99, 102, 103
**Cover Credits:** The Cathedral milosk50/
**Shutterstock**

**Distribution**
**UK, Ireland and Europe:** Apa Publications (UK)
Ltd; sales@roughguides.com
**United States and Canada:** Ingram Publisher
Services; ips@ingramcontent.com
**Australia and New Zealand:** Booktopia;
retailer@booktopia.com.au
**Worldwide:** Apa Publications (UK) Ltd;
sales@roughguides.com

**Special Sales, Content Licensing
and CoPublishing**
Rough Guides can be purchased in bulk
quantities at discounted prices. We can create
special editions, personalised jackets and
corporate imprints tailored to your needs. sales@
roughguides.com; http://roughguides.com

**Contact us**
Every effort has been made to provide accurate
information in this publication, but changes
are inevitable. The publisher cannot be held
responsible for any resulting loss, inconvenience
or injury sustained by any traveller as a result
of information or advice contained in the
guide. We would appreciate it if readers would
call our attention to any errors or outdated
information, or if you feel we've left something
out. Please send your comments with the
subject line "Rough Guide Mini Porto Update" to
mail@uk.roughguides.com.